BRITISH
PARACHUTES

Jean-Louis Perquin

CONTENTS

A Norwegian paratrooper of the independent parachutist coy, with a Type X parachute. His legs are flexed for the landing.
(Forsvarsmuseet Oslo)

MILITARY PARACHUTES

Freedom come from the sky

I was born in a workshop
Assembled by weary hands
Silk gown I won't be
I only want to serve the Paras.

In silk canvas I am folded
Soon I will take flight
On a back like a parasol
To save occupied France.

I am a bit of freedom
By men hardly won
Resist, I am here with you!
Victory is before us.

This poem written by the school "le clos de la Ferme de Torcy" (Scinc et Marne) won the 2008 André Maginot public-spirit and memory prize in the elementary school category.

Above from left to right.
Stick of trainees emplaning on a Whitley in August 1942 at Ringway. They wear Bungey training helmets.
(Airborne Forces Museum)

August 1942, a stick of the Parachute Regiment ready to emplane into a Whitley. They wear Mk 1 Type X parachutes, some with dark, others with light kaki outer packs.
(IWM)

Opposite.
Memorial at the entrance of Tatton Park, legendary DZ of Parachute Training Schools n°1 (PTS), ex Central Landing Establishment (CLE), at Ringway.
(Airborne Forces Museum)

Until 1939, the British do not intend to parachute troops and no specific equipment exists. The only existing paratrooper training center is a school of the RAF based at Henlow in charge of the instruction and the training of crews in the use of rescue parachute. The canopy of this Irvin rescue parachute being of insufficient dimension (24 ft of diameter), the rate of fall remains too high and causes numerous wounds. Accordingly, a more important canopy of 28 ft of diameter is adopted for training and drill.

In 1940, in particular during the seizing of the fort of Eben-Emael in Belgium (10 to 11 May 1940), the German operations demonstrate the utility of the vertical assault by the parachutists. Churchill reacts and demands that the United Kingdom quickly gets a body of 5000 parachutists at disposal. On 21 June 1940, the ministry of the Air creates the first school (Central Landing School, CLS) based on the civil airport of Manchester at Ringway, which was seen as non-strategic within the general pattern of the Battle of England.

Squadron Leader Louis Strange DSO MC DFC is appointed at the head of the school. He quickly realizes that he needs a second airfield to face the number of

Opposite.
Aerial view on Tatton Park DZ in 2005. 60 000 parachutists from several nations will make their first jump here. For special missions they were trained over pools, others over wooden areas. 383 000 jumps from planes or balloons were performed until 1946.
(Airborne Forces Museum)

trainees he has to form. Strange gets in touch with another pioneer of aviation, Lord Maurice Egerton, 4th and last baron of Tatton. Egerton owns an estate which seems to fit the purpose and the man lives only 5 miles south of Ringway. On 6 July, Strange visits the place and lord Egerton grants him the right to use Tatton Park as his main jumping zone.

With an exceeding sense of patriotism as well as fair play, Lord Egerton will accept all the requirements of the parachutists to assure the training of roughly 60 000 parachutists. The configuration of Tatton Park also allows special trainees to make jumps on pools or on wooden areas. The length of the zone allows the planes to release, at 800 feet of height, 10 then 20 parachutists at each passage. 383 000 jumps out of planes or balloons are realized until 1946!

Strange also has to find instructors. In 1940, the only British technicians who have an actual knowledge of the functioning of a parachute are those of Henlow. A

Above.
Last briefing before emplaning. This kind of leather helmets were worn during the early jumps. The outer pack is dark and the harness white.
(IWM)

Opposite.
RAF Instructor sergeant with his observer's harness equipped with a chest parachute.
(RAF Museum)

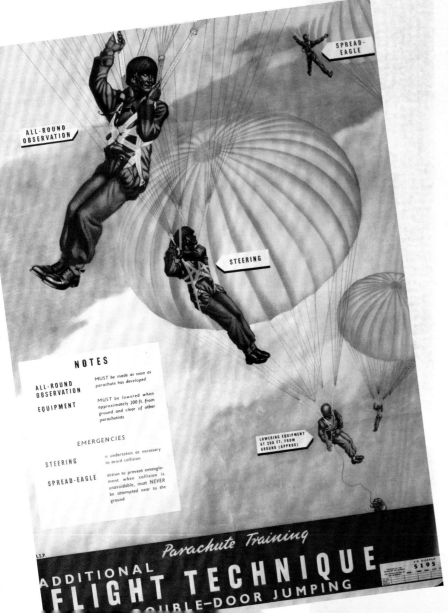

first detachment of eight voluntary specialists is sent to Ringway. Twenty other Army volunteers arrive as well as some civil professionals, exhibition paratroopers, who have joined the RAF. Two instructors are quickly going to distinguish themselves by creating methods and techniques that are sometimes still in use: Harry Ward and John C. Kilkenny, who joined the school in October, 1941. The latter conceives a full program of training and drill with appropriate apparatus. This system is known in history under the naming of Kilkenny Circus. A Polish instructor, the Flight lieutenant Julian Gebolys, discovers how to reduce balancing and speed or to give direction to the parachute by steering properly the shoulder lift webs.

If the instructors are ready, there still is need of trainees to test the concept and take an initial training course. On 9 July 1940 Troops B and C of N°2 Commando are chosen.

The first attempts are made with dummies equipped with Irvin parachutes without rescue parachute. The first real jumps are realized on 13 July 1940 by 8 instructors of the RAF equipped with parachutes Irvin. Dropped by bombers Amstrong Whitworth Whitley, the first two ones jump from a platform put in place of the back machine gun turret, the six following ones from an opening made in the floor of the fuselage. Jumping from the back platform turns out to be particularly dangerous and the technique is given up. The next day, on 14 July, it is the first six trainees' turn to jump, but they are dropped from the opening on the floor. Only one of them gets injured.

The parachute Irvin presents numerous shortcomings. On 25 July 1940, while already 135 jumps have been made, a Commando squad, R Evans, crashes in the ground, his parachute not having opened correctly. This first fatal accident puts an end to the tests.

The association of two British manufacturers, GQ and Irvin Air Chutes, is going to help things move again. GQ was created in 1932 when James Gregory and Raymond Quilter joined to compete with the company Irvin on the market of the rescue parachutes of Royal Air Forces.

In 1936, GQ unsuccessfully proposed to the war ministry a military parachute for the British troops. After the accidents of July 1940, at the Central Landing Establishment (CLE) of the RAF at Ringway, Raymond Quilter submits again his model «Statichute» developed in association with Leslie Irvin.

Above.
Close up on a parachutist pulling on the lift webs. This technique, which allows to impulse a horizontal direction to the parachute, was discovered by a polish instructor, the Flight lieutenant Julian Gebolys.
(Airborne Forces Museum)

Opposite.
Jump from a Whitley at Ringway.
(IWM)

Opposite.
25 May 1941 demonstration jumps from a Whitley in front of King Georges VI at Windsor.
(IWM)

Below.
During the first jumping session on 13 July 1940, the first two ones jumped from a platform put in place of the back machine gun turret of an Amstrong Whitworth Whitley. It turns out to be particularly dangerous and the technique is given up. Their equipment was of a very early kind: leather helmets, no parachutist jacket and no gaiters.
(IWM)

The automatic opening system is adopted, activated by a Static Line of 12 foot 6 inch hung on a fixed point of the plane. Quickly this fixed hanging point is replaced by an Anchor Line Cable where several static lines can be fixed. The bag in the back of the parachutist opens according to a precise sequence: static line, bag, rigging lines then canopy. The Statichute proposed by the company created by James Gregory and Raymond Quilter (G.Q) is definitively adopted. This system of opening, known as «suspension lines first », decreases the risks of incidents thanks to the permanent tension of the sct canopy suspension lines, also called rigging lines. It also allows a softer opening for the parachutist, unlike the "canopy first" of the previous parachutes. In close collaboration with the CLE and after 500 tries with dummies, the first jumps with living parachutists take place successfully on 8 August 1940. This parachute is approved under the label of Type X Mk I and will be in use during the whole war.

The American parachute T-5 works is based on the opposite principle: the canopy is spread and the parachutist falls until the complete deployment of the suspension lines, which causes a rough opening. The American parachute includes a front rescue parachute, unlike the Type X since the British consider that war jumps at low height do not allow its use.

A volunteer parachutist of the 2d commando at Tatton park in 1941.
(IWM)

Opposite.
Dropping of Norwegian parachutists from a Whitley.
(Forsvarsmuseet Oslo)

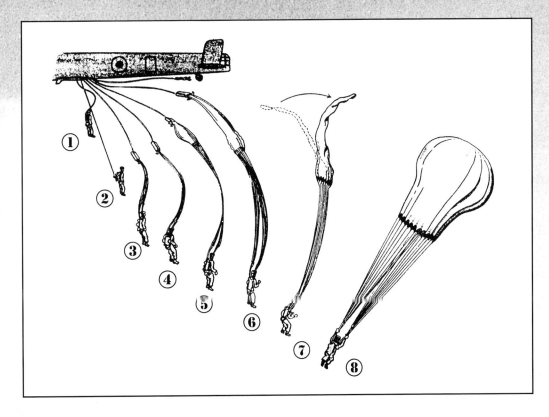

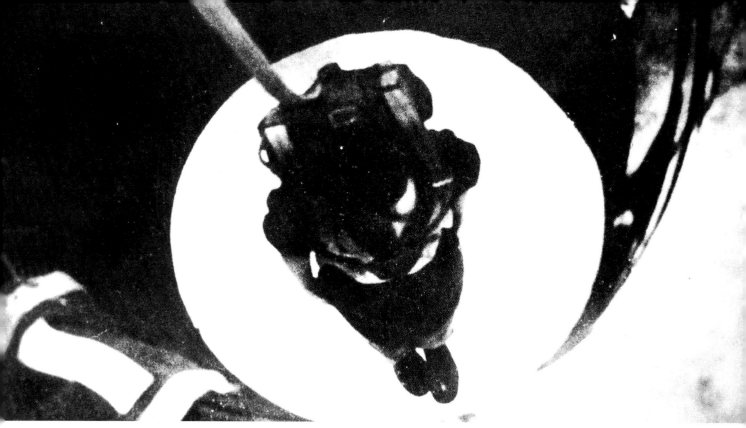

Above.
Outclass jump from a balloon hole. The man and the statict line make a perfect line.
(IWM)

Opposite.
Parachutists from the side door of a C 47. The different stages of the opening of the Type X parachute can be clearly observed.
(MoD)

Below.
A Captain from the Parachute regiment and a RAF staff sergeant display the opening of the Type X parachute. The main outer pack still is relied to the harness worn by the staff sergeant while the inner bag is still carried by the Captain. The rigging lines have started to uncoil. The canopy will get out from the outer pack, with its vented relied by the tie to a string that will break when the tension gets at its maximum. The parachutist will be released free while the inner bag and the static line remain bound to the aircraft anchorage.
(Airborne Forces Museum)

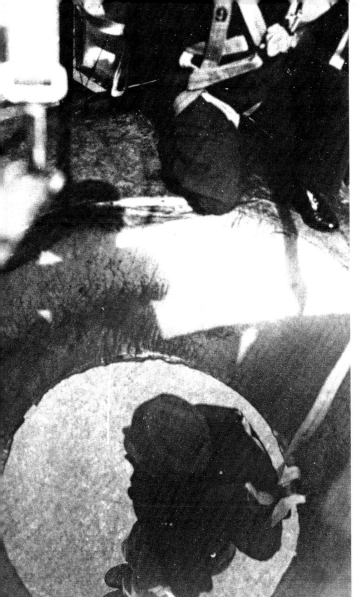

Above from left to right.
Nice exit of a trainee from a balloon hole.
(IWM)

**The parachutist has just jumped from the plane.
The static line is fully uncoiled and the inner**
bag starting to get out of the outer pack.
(IWM)

Opposite.
**Men of the 6th Royal Welsh regiment embarking
on a balloon at Tatton Park in August 1942.**
(Airborne Forces Museum)

At the same time, it is decided to train part of the trainee in the use of gliders. In September 1940, the Central Landing School (CLS) becomes the Central Landing Establishment (CLE) organized in 3 entities: Parachute Squadron, Gilder Squadron and Technical Development Unit. During the first two months, 350 trainees are qualified in spite of 50 failures due to the wounds, including several fatal accidents.

In November 1940 the instructors put at test before adopting the jump from balloon. On 21 November 1940 the commando squads of troops B and C become N°11 Special Air Service Battalion. They are not to be confused with the SAS issued from the «L» Detachment of Special Air Brigade established in July 1941, in Western Desert, by Captain David Stirling, that have become internationally renowned.

At the end of 1940, about 2000 jumps have been realized by the men of the N°11 Special Air service Battalion.

In April 1941 two balloons are available at Tatton Park and every trainee makes his first 2 jumps since this vector.

On 9 July 1941, Group Captain Maurice Newnham DFC, is named at the head of the Central Landing Establishment, CLE, which changes its naming and becomes N°1 Parachute training School (PTS)

To face the need in reconditioning of parachutes at Ringway, a shed is transformed into room of folding.

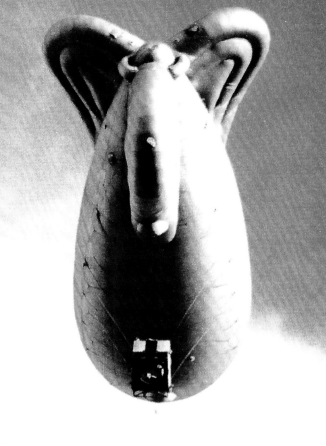

Opposite.
Nice view of a Type X parachute with its camouflaged canopy uncoiled under the jump balloon at Tatton Park.
(IWM)

The folding of parachutes is entrusted to British young women, the WAAF (Women Auxillary Air Forces).

The WAAF will fold 429 000 parachutes during the war.

In February 1943, on 92 000 actual jumps, mainly at Tatton Park, only 26 lethal accidents had happened. They had been mainly caused by problems of suspension lines and only one was granted to a problem of folding.

Opposite.
Women Air Auxiliary Forces (WAAF) at work over packing tables. The Mk I Type X parachutes on the ground have a dark outer pack of an early version. A cautionary notice reminds them: «Remember a man's life depends on every parachute you pack».
(IWM)

Below.
Parachute Training School (PTS) Ringway 1944, seven members of the WAAF, each with over two and a half year service at the Parachute Training School, display the Mk II Type X they have packed themselves. Left to right: ACW1 Sheina Brown (25) of Covent Grove, Glasgow (formerly a saleswoman); ACW1 Edith Tindle (26) of Shotton Colliery, County Durham (formerly a cinema attendant); ACW1 Olive Snow (23) of Knutsford, Cheshire (formerly a mill worker); Cpl Doris Mothersole (29) of Chesham, Buckinghamshire, (formerly a laundry hand); Sergeant Betty Jones (24) of Pontefract, Yorkshire (formerly a housekeeper); LACW Phyllis Baduchowska (21) (the English wife of a Polish paratrooper); and ACW1 Anne Douglas of Liverpool (formerly a tailoress). (IWM)

Below.
Kilkenny Circus: Drill jump from the airframe of a Whitley, used to let the trainees jump from the hole of a bomber. The Mk I Type X parachutes with dark outer packs are of an early fabrication.
(Public Archives Canada)

SMALL AND LARGE TYPE "A" PARACHUTES

It is the most mythical parachute, used by the Special Services and abandoned because of the excessive large number of accidents. It remains a riddle for the specialists. Only the testimonies of some of the agents who have used this type of parachute have reached until us, as well as some pieces of harnesses. The understanding of its functioning has been improved by the discovery in the archives of an Air Ministry report of October 1942 on Specialized Supplies Dropping Apparatus. Developed jointly to the Type X, the Type A is intended for the special operations when only 2 or 3 paras are to be dropped. The A pack contains a parachute and a supplies to be dropped. The static line is a flexible steel cable extension of 16 ft. The parachute is contained in large pack suspended inside the aircraft above the floor aperture with the ends of the lift straps attached to the modified observer type harness worn by the parachutist. Its main peculiarity is that the supplies Pack is attached at each side to a snap hook fitted to each lift strap, so as to be suspended between the parachute rigging lines and the parachutist during the descent. The design was based on the parachutes used by balloon crewmembers during the 1st World War.

Above.
An agent ready to jump from a Whitley bomber, equipped with a Type A parachute. Notice the RAF "Observer's" type of harness with its straps attached to a bag containing the canopy, the rigging lines as well as a supplies pack. The A pack is suspended inside the aircraft above the floor aperture. The static line is made of a 16 ft long flexible steel cable which follows a complex pattern when uncoiling.
(Airborne Forces Museum)

Above.
In 1890, Kate Paulus was the first woman ever to pack her own parachute. She did over 150 jumps and died aged 67 in 1935. The filiation leading to the Type A parachute is obvious.
(Robert Lenoir Collection)

Opposite.
A German observer jumping from a balloon in 1916.
(Robert Lenoir collection)

The type A packs are made in two sizes, the A large and the A small. The standard camouflage canopy measures 28 ft in diameter and is known as "small A" when the "large A" is 32 feet large with a 2 ft apex. Apart from the dimensions, the only difference is in the size of the canopy used with each and the number of their rigging lines. The canopy of the small A type (Ø28 ft) displays 28 panels with 28 rigging lines of 400 lb resistance each. The canopy of the large A type (Ø32 ft) has 28 or 32 panels, and the same number of rigging lines. The apex of the canopy (Ø2 ft) is similar on the two types.

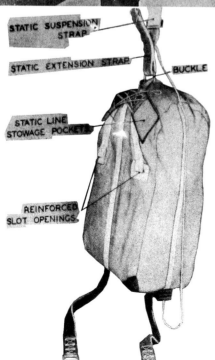

STATIC SUSPENSION STRAP

STATIC EXTENSION STRAP

BUCKLE

STATIC LINE STOWAGE POCKET

REINFORCED SLOT OPENINGS

Above.
STS 15 b: located on the Natural History Museum of London, this room is dedicated to the production to the agents designed for a mission of all the equipment specific to the SOE. At the bottom, a mannequin on a jumpsuit is hanging to a camouflaged canopy. According to the bag above it, it has to be a Type A!
(National Archives)

Opposite.
Close up on the A pack with its suspension system to the anchorage bar fixed on the ceiling of the plane body.
(From: Specialized Supplies Dropping Apparatus, Air Ministry, October 1942)

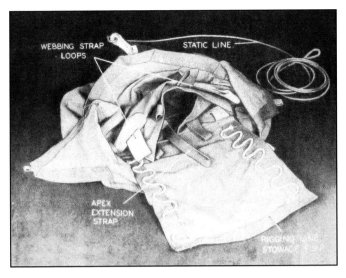

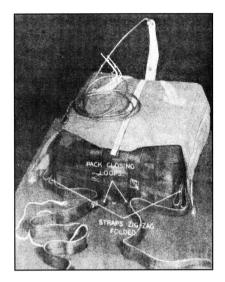

Opposite from left to right.
Inner view of an A pack showing the different canvas flaps allowing to store the canopy and the supplies pack and to stowe the rigging lines.

An A pack. The supplies pack is now set inside, the four external flaps remain to be folded to finish the packing.
(From: Specialized Supplies Dropping Apparatus, Air Ministry, October 1942)

Below.
Inner view of an A pack. The canopy is packed and stowed at its place, the two canvas flaps are folded to protect it from the supplies pack. The rigging lines are stored and maintained by the double row of bungee cords.
(From: Specialized Supplies Dropping Apparatus, Air Ministry, October 1942)

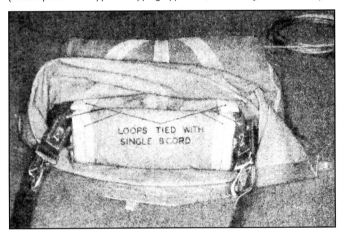

Opposite.
Picture allowing to figure out the length of the 15 ft lift webs and to see the two hooks allowing to fix the supplies pack.
(From: Specialized Supplies Dropping Apparatus, Air Ministry, October 1942)

Operation and description

The parachutist carries the modified harness of a RAF observer. Two lift straps of 15 ft are coupled to a pack hanging above him and the exit pit. The supplies pack is contained in the lower part of the bag, the rigging lines folded in the higher part with the canopy maintained by two flaps.

The harness is green with a black centerline stitching. It contains two characteristic hooks at the end of the straps and all the metal part are painted in green. When the parachutist jumps, the lift straps are extended causing the release pin to be pulled out from the cons. This allows the complete pack to fall through the floor aperture to the extent of the static line. A pack falls after the parachutist through the exit hole. The weight

Below.
Straps hook of the Type A parachute harness found in Norway (Picture Stein Aasland). These hooks can also be seen on the pictures of the harness of Tony Brooks worn by René Citerne.
(Stein Aasland)

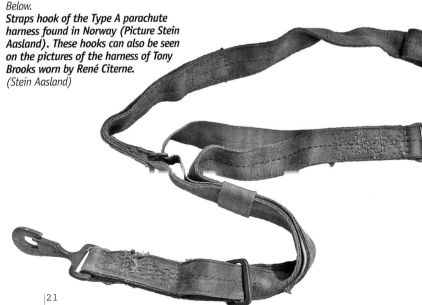

of the parachutist breaks the cord tie at the mouth of the pack cover and the supplies and the parachute are pulled from the pack cover which remains attached to the aircraft by the static lines.

Above.
Type A Quick Release Box found in Norway, with fabric number 5823.
(Stein Aasland)

Opposite.
Quick Release Box from a Type A harness found in Norway. The harness is green with black topstitch and all the metallic parts are painted in green.
(Stein Aasland)

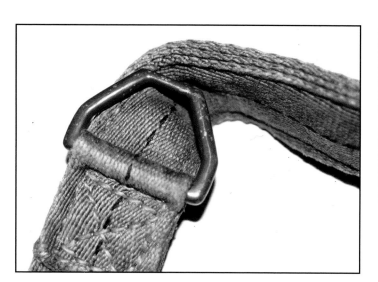

Left opposite.
Close up on one of the Two « D » rings on the Type A parachute harness found in Norway.
(Stein Aasland)

Right opposite.
Two « D » rings on the Type A parachute harness found in Norway.
(Stein Aasland)

Opposite.
Lift webs bound to one set of seven camouflaged rigging lines belonging to the Type A parachute found in Norway.
(Stein Aasland)

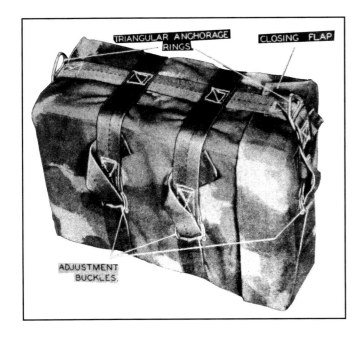

Supplies Pack

Once the parachute is open, the agent is hanging under the canopy with his Supplies Pack holding to the lift webs by two triangular hooks above his head. This peculiar parachute turns to be most useful when fragile equipment has to be delivered because once the agent is on the ground, the canopy will land very gently since it then only supports between 40 and 60 lbs.

Actually the pack is a camouflaged cotton bag usually containing a radio protected in a hair lok box. The whole is tightly maintained thanks to a harness made of 3 adaptable parts, with 0,13 ft broad straps. Two nickel-plated triangular rings in the higher part are to be relied to the hooks at the upper ends of the lift webs. Meant for the dropping from plane, the complex and delicate Type A proves to be rather unreliable when used from a fast moving aircraft. Several mortal incidents and injuries happen. During the opening, the load can come to hurt the parachutist strongly enough to cause him wounds. At the collision then, some suspension lines are not stretched out and can get tangled. The parachute then turns into a torch or the feet of the parachutist are trapped, making him fall on the head. Such is the case of two agents of the BCRA, Edgar Tupet Thome blindly parachuted during the night of 0 December 1941 and Jean Ayral, in July 1942.

Many researches are undertaken to make this parachute completely reliable but no solution is found as long as the load remains above the parachutist. Eventually, the load is fixed with a parachute to the harness of the parachutist. Linked with the harness by a static line of 40 feet, it is released by the agent himself. Experience shows that a parachute of 12 feet is perfectly adapted for this type of load.

In his memories published in December 1952 under the title of « Two eggs on my plate » a Norwegian SIS veteran by the name of Oluf Reed Olsen gave some more details on the complex operation of this parachute which he used during the night of 19 to 20 April 1943. When he jumped, the 15 ft lift webs linking the harness to the bundle get tightened and pulled the bundle which then went more or less straight through the hole. The top of the parachute was hooked to a 16 ft steel cable. The man-bundle assembly first fell from the length of the steel cable which then pulled the parachute for its total 30 ft length.

In summary, the complete sequence meant that the parachutist would experience a 62 ft fall before the breaking string would give way under the weight and his parachute was completely open: 15 ft for the straps, then 16 ft for the steel cable and finally 30 ft for the canopy!

The equipment bags would add another 89 libs, with a 70 lb useful load, comprising two handguns, several civilian suits, two days of rations in a watertight container (RAF rations composed of condensed food, chocolate, raisins, etc) and of course a radio set.

Above from left to right.
Full supplies pack of a Type A. The camouflaged canvas pack is consolidated by a harness made of three flat straps. Two triangular rings allow to bind the pack to the hooks that have been added at the end of the lift webs.
(From: Specialized Supplies Dropping Apparatus, Air Ministry, October 1942)

Supplies pack reconstituted with its cover marked "HAWT-DORN B" and a harness found in East of France.
(Picture by Philippe Chapillon, collection of Laurent Jacquet)

NOTE POUR LE CAPITAINE BIENVENUE.

OBJET : MISSION ROACH/MACKEREL.

Les dispositions suivantes ont été prises pour l'emballage des effets personnels, postes radio et machines à écrire qu'emportent les agents ROACH et MACKEREL :

1. ROACH MAJOR sautera avec un large "A" contenant ses vêtements et le poste ROACH ALPHA.

2. ROACH MINOR sautera avec un small "A" contenant le poste ROACH et les lampes de réception.

3. MACKEREL sautera avec un "statichute".

4. En plus il y aura un paquet contenant :

Les vêtements de ROACH MINOR.

Les vêtements de MACKEREL.

Le poste MACKEREL (dans la valise de MACKEREL)

3 machines à écrire (une de ces machines sera dans la valise de ROACH MINOR.)

soit un total de :

3 postes radios (petit modèle)
3 valises de vêtements
3 machines à écrire
4 lampes de réception avec piles, etc. de rechange

Les agents sauteront dans l'ordre démontré ci-dessus. (sauf que le paquet pourrait être largué d'abord, dépendant de son poids et de la vitesse du vent sur le point d'atterrissage.)

O.L.T.

Roach/Mackerel mission parachuting instructions

BCRA memo 644/FF dated 23 June 1942, addressed to Captain Bienvenue:
Roach Major will jump with a large "A" holding his clothes and Roach Alpha's radio set;
Roach Minor will jump with a small "A" holding Roach's radio set as well as the reception lamps;
- Mackerel will jump with a "statichute";
In addition, a bundle will hold the following:
- Roach Minor's clothes,
- Mackerel's clothes,
- Mackerel's radio set (in Mackerel's suitcase),
- Three typewriters (one will be placed in Roach Minor's suitcase).
Total:
- 3 radio sets (small),
- 3 suitcases filled with clothes,
- 3 typewriters
- 4 reception lamps complete with spare batteries.
The agent will jump in the above-mentioned sequence. The general equipment pack may be dropped first, depending on its weight and on the wind speed on the landing zone.

Above.
Note from the BCRA dated from 23 June 1942, with parachuting instructions for the Roach/Mackerel mission. No less than three different types of parachutes are quoted, with a small A, a large A and a Statichute (Type X)! *(SHD)*

Below.
Another supplies pack cover found in France. It is also marked on two sides with stenciled white letters: "HAWT DORN B".
((Picture by and collection of Laurent Jacquet)

Below.
Side view of the supplies pack cover marked 1935.
(Collection of Jordan Mathan, picture by the author)

This memo confirms the existence of two canopy sizes (Small A and Large A) and it illustrates the fact that three different kinds of parachutes could be used on the same drop.

This mission was dropped one month later, on 25 July 1942, by a 138 Squadron Halifax piloted by Flight Lieutenant Wodzicki on DZ "Moge" near Coursages, 10 km South West of Montluçon in the Allier department. The real names of the agents of this team were Jean Ayral (Compagnon de la Libération) a.k.a. Pal and his radio operators François Briant a.k.a Pal-W and Daniel Bouyjou-Cordier (Compagnon de la Libération) a.k.a. Bip-W.

Roach Major who had jumped with a Large "A" landed on his head, his feet caught in the rigging lines, a quite common occurrence with the Type "A":

15 February 1941 Maurice Duclos a.k.a. St Jacques broke both legs on landing,

7 August 1941, G. Turck belonging to the SOE/F Corsican network got injured on landing,

9 December 1941, Edgard Tupet-Thomé from the BCRA landed on his head, his feet caught in the rigging lines and his radio operator Joseph Piet has a leg broken,

1 May 1942, Lucien Montet from the BCRA got injured on landing,

29 May 1942, a radio operator from the BCRA was killed on landing near Saint Etienne,

1 July 1942, Tony Brooks landed horizontaly…

26 July 1942, Orabona, a radio operator from the BCRA, broke both his legs and crushed his thorax on landing ; he died the next day,

31 July 1942, two SOE/F agents, Claude de Baissac and Henry Peulevé got injured on the landing,

17 November 1942, Gustave Bieler, from SOE/F, injured his spine while landing.

It seems that the decision not to use Type "A" anymore was taken during 1943.

Below.
Hair lok box and its cover intended for protecting supplies bundles of small size. *(From: Specialized Supplies Dropping Apparatus, Air Ministry, October 1942)*

Type « A » General Equipment Pack (GEP)

Meant to parachute heavier and bigger extra equipment, it is composed with an equipment pack linked to a parachute, with a rather similar pattern to Type "A" parachute.

A quick release box painted in green keeps closed the four flaps of the lower opening on the camouflaged canvas pack carrying the load. The QRB is protected by a wooden hemisphere which hits the ground first. A wooden locking cruch plate, tied to the bag by a cord, prevents any ill-timed opening of the bag.

On a back strap, a cone with a pin allows an instant releasing during the parachute's opening sequence (quick release system of "pin and cone" type).

The harness is made of straps 1' ¾" wide and 3000 lb of resistance. On each side of the upper part of the harness a nickel triangular ring bounds the pack to the hooks of the parachute lift webs. All reinforcements are made with green parts of harness and the metal parts are painted green, with the exception of two nickel-plated rings fixing the lift webs.

When the general equipment pack is thrown out of the aircraft, it falls freely until the static line is fully extended when the parachute pack is pulled out of the pack. Simultaneously, the release cord pulls the release pin out of the anchorage cone thus permitting the wooden locking cruch plate to be pulled from the quick-release unit by the cord elastic.

When the pack reaches the ground, the wooden hemisphere first makes contact, is depressed and operates the quick-release unit which frees the ends of the four webbing straps ready for the withdrawal of the pack contents.

The maximum size of the packs that can be dropped are 25 x 25 x 40 inch by the hole in the plane belly and 30x20x30 inch by the door. The size of the parachute and the number of rigging lines are adapted to the total loaded weight which can vary from 40 to 240 lb.

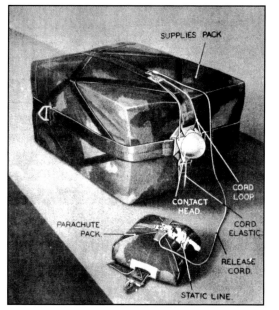

Opposite.
General Equipment Pack meant to drop additional equipment, heavier and larger. Its whole weight can vary from 40 to 240 lb. It actually consists of a camouflaged canvas pack connected to a parachute, on a close system to the Type A parachute. The camouflaged canvas pack where the equipment is loaded contains a low aperture with four flaps closing with a green painted QRB. The box is protected by a wooden cone intended to hit the ground first.
(From: Specialized Supplies Dropping Apparatus, Air Ministry, October 1942)

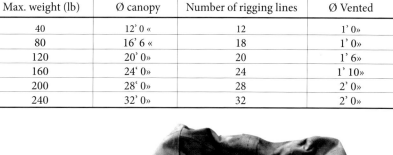

Max. weight (lb)	Ø canopy	Number of rigging lines	Ø Vented
40	12' 0 «	12	1' 0»
80	16' 6 «	18	1' 0»
120	20' 0»	20	1' 6»
160	24' 0»	24	1' 10»
200	28' 0»	28	2' 0»
240	32' 0»	32	2' 0»

Opposite.
This bag related to the belongings of Captain Jumeau is very close to General Equipment Pack version. No other one has ever been identified. The bag is made with the same kind of Jacob camouflaged cotton canvas in use for SOE equipment. The harness straps are directly sewn on the bag. The quick release box painted in green keeps closes the four flaps. The wooden locking cruch plate, tied to the bag by a cord, is still there.
(Military Museum of Périgueux, picture by the author)

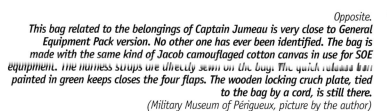

The General Equipment Pack of British Captain Clément Marc Jumeau

a.k.a. Robert, a.k.a. Reporter is kept on the Military Museum of Perigueux.

This SOE/F officer was dropped during the Corsican mission, near Villamblard, during the night of 10 to 11 October 1941 by a RAF 138 squadron Whitley bomber piloted by Flight Lieutenant Jackson. Are also involved in this mission Captaine Jack Bereford Hayes (Eric, Corsican), and Lieutenants Jean Philippe Le Harivel (Hiccup) and Daniel Turberville (Diviner).

This early parachuting involves an undoubtedly experimental equipment that one can discover at the Museum: a jacket and jumping trousers close to the early jumping suit, but clearly different, with no snap fasteners on the lower part of the leg to tie the spare bag nor snaps at the waist. In the same way, one can observe a bag very much similar to the General Equipment Pack. Its operating system is exactly the same except that the harness is directly stitched to the bag and that both connecting nickel rings are not triangular. In every way it is a unique piece of equipment!

In August 1942, Jumeau drifts to Spain in the company of Bégué, P. Bloch, le Harivel, Hayes, Roche and F. Garel (Bouguennec). Arrested at Figueras, they're interned at Miranda camp before reaching London. Volunteer on a second mission, Jumeau lives out an Halifax hit by the Flack. Imprisoned in Germany, Jumeau dies on 26 March 1944 out of lack of medical care.

Opposite.
**Jumpsuit belonging to Captain Clément Marc JUMEAU, a.k.a. « Robert », a. k. a. « REPORTER ». This sabotage instructor was dropped from Whitley bomber of the RAF 138 squadron piloted by Flight lieutenant Jackson, in the same time than Jack B Hayes, a.k.a. Corsican, Jean Ph. Le Harivel and Daniel Turberville, at Villamblard (hamlet of Puyauderie) on the night of 10 to 11 October 1941. Jumeau was arrested less than 10 days later. During a second mission, he died in prison on 26 March 1944.
This camouflaged jumpsuit is made of a jacket and suits, not of a single overall. It is a discovery since no other jumpsuit of this kind had ever been observed until now. It seems to have been an early version or even an experimental try, which gives it a thrilling historical interest.
(Military Museum of Périgueux, picture by the author)*

Opposite.
Close up on the open General Equipment Pack, whose four flaps are closed over the Quick Release Box. *(Military Museum of Périgueux, picture by the author)*

Opposite.
Back side of the bag of Captain Jumeau, which allows to see two nickel rings rather typical of the air material from the beginning of the war, as well as a strap with a "pin and cone" type of quick release system.
(Military Museum of Périgueux, picture by the author)

Ci-dessous.
Close up on the strap sewn at the bottom of the bag with the "pin and cone" type of quick release system.
(Military Museum of Périgueux, picture by the author)

Opposite.
Front view of the green painted Quick Release Box of the General Equipment Pack.
(Military Museum of Périgueux, picture by the author)

Below.
The registration number of the QRB is 7452, not that far from the 5823 number of the Type A box found in Norway.
(Military Museum of Périgueux, picture by the author)

Opposite.
Side view of the wooden locking crutch plate designed to fit to the Quick release box in order to secure further its closing.
(Military Museum of Périgueux, picture by the author)

Opposite.
Hair lok box intended for protecting supplies bundle of large size.
(From: Specialized Supplies Dropping Apparatus, Air Ministry, October 1942)

Inquiry and testimonies

To this day, no complete type « A » parachute has been found. Our understanding can only be improved thanks to:

- The October 1942 Air Ministry report.

- Some pieces of the harness remaining, through pictures and oral or written testimonies.

- Some elements of a harness, unfortunately incomplete, found and identified by Lcl Aasland. The harness is green, the case of the quick release box and all the buckles set painted in green. Two specific hooks can be found at the end of the extension cable and two rings, with their typical D shape, are sewn to the harness;

- The General Equipment Pack of Captain Jumeau, on display at the Military Museum of Périgueux;

- Pictures belonging to Citerne family, on one of which it can be seen that the harness is not white (thus presumably green) with the same kind of rings, rather peculiar, than on the harness found in Norway.

In 2005, François Chatelin, who used to be part of the reception team of Marco polo network, reveals during an interview that on 4 June 1942, just after landing, he was greeted by Pierre Brossolette complaining "On the opening, I almost got the luggage on my face", which means he must have used a Type "A" parachute.

In November 2011, on another interview with the author, Edgard Tupet-Thomé from the BCRA positively recognized the Type "A" of a parachutist on water-

Above.
Albert Rigoulet and his mother standing before the remaining of the first dropping of agents carried out with marking on the ground, on the night of 10 to 11 October 1941. The camouflaged canopy can be seen, as well as a Sorbo helmet hanging from the door of the barn where the parachutists slept on the first night.
(Collection Jean- Michel Rémy)

Opposite.
Profile picture where one can see the line of snap fasteners at the bottom of the left leg and the collar of the jumpsuit. It is fairly obvious yet that young René Citerne has been unable to don the harness correctly. *(Citerne, Bruno Barthelot collection)*

colors as being the same kind of parachute he had to jump on 9 December 1941.

Daniel Cordier, radio operator and secretary of Jean Moulin, whose jump has already been quoted with the Roach/Mackerel mission, has no memory to have ever jumped with a bag on his back (like with the Type X), neither at Tattoon Park, nor on his operational jump on 25 July 1942 (Interview with the author, 2009).

According to the pictures of the period, in 1942 both Robert Sheppard (SOE/F Spruce) and Tony Brooks (SOE/F Pimento) have jumped with camouflaged canopy parachutes, the first one on 2 June, the second one during the night of 1 to 2 July. There's no doubted that Tony Brooks, who actually fell horizontally, jumped with a Type "A", as testify the already mentioned pictures of the Citerne family.

Opposite.
During the night of 2 June 1942, Bob Sheppard was dropped from an Halifax of the RAF 138 squadron piloted by the Flight/Lieutenant Walczak. The camouflaged canopy of his parachute remained stuck on the roof of the Gendarmerie in the town of Anse in the Rhone department.
(Mairie d'Anse)

Below.
Tony Morris Brooks, alias « Alphone », created the Pimento circuit on behalf of the SOE F section. Dropped "blind" on the night of 1 to 2 July 1942 close to Bas Soleil castle, 2,49 miles North of St Léonard de Noblat (department of Haute Vienne), he landed flat and would not have survived if he had not fallen on a tree and hurt his leg.
Brooks had been instructed to establish liaison with the CGT, a communist trading union, and to act as technical assistant to René Berholet. He was also to endeavour to direct the energies of members of the CGT into a coordinated plan, to train and equip them, firstly to do sabotage by long-term means, and secondly to do active sabotage on vital supplies and thirdly to cooperate actively in D-Day operations.
Although extremely young (he was the youngest officer ever dropped by F section into the field), Captain Brooks succeeded admirably in straining all these objectives.
His success can be understood by the results of his action on the single year of 1944.
April: grease sabotage on 82 bogied tank-carrying wagons belonging to Das Reich, Deutschland and Der Fuehrer divisions in Montauban marshalling yards.
June: 78 steam and 29 electric locomotives were destroyed.
Early September: Major Brooks led the first American tank patrol into Lyons as far as the Rhone and placed himself at the disposal of Lt-col. Head of Special Force Unit-4 in Lyons.
On the whole, the Pimento circuit received 70 droppings of weapons, ammunitions, explosives, spread on a large area. Committees created by Brooks proved reliable and the operations ordered by Pimento were easily granted by the RAF for they were known to have been planned on safe landing zones.
The success of the circuit owed much to the quality of its relations with the CGT, especially the railway unions, as well as to the organization of its circuit in groups under leaders who were in contact with him only through cut-outs or post-boxes.
On completion of his duties, major Brooks returned to England and was awarded the Distinguished Service Order and Croix de Guerre with Palms. (He already had the Military Cross).
(From : report of the SOE F Pimento circuit)

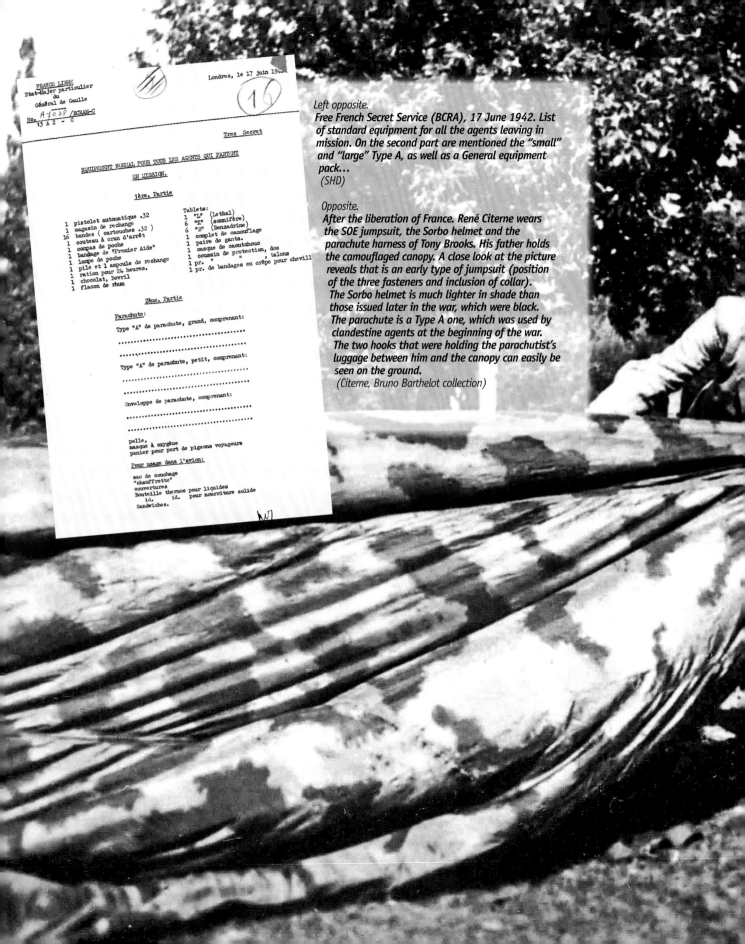

FRANCE LIBRE
Etat-Major particulier
du
Général de Gaulle
No. A 7038 /BCRAM-C
13 A 2 - C

Londres, le 17 Juin 194.

16

Très Secret

EQUIPEMENT NORMAL POUR TOUS LES AGENTS QUI PARTENT

EN MISSION.

1ère. Partie

1 pistolet automatique .32
1 magasin de rechange
16 bandes (cartouches .32)
1 couteau à cran d'arrêt
1 compas de poche
1 bandage de "Premier Aide"
1 lampe de poche
1 pile et 1 ampoule de rechange
1 ration pour 24 heures.
1 chocolat, Bovril
1 flacon de rhum

Tablets:
1 "L" (Lethal)
6 "K" (sommifère)
6 "B" (Benzadrine)
1 complet de camouflage
1 paire de gants.
1 casque de caoutchouc
1 coussin de protection, dos
1 pr. " " , talons
1 pr. de bandages en crêpe pour chevill

2ème. Partie

Parachute:

Type "A" de parachute, grand, comprenant:
....

Type "A" de parachute, petit, comprenant:
....

Enveloppe de parachute, comprenant:
....
....

pelle,
masque à oxygène
panier pour port de pigeons voyageurs

Pour usage dans l'avion:

sac de couchage
"chauffrette"
couvertures
Bouteille thermos pour liquides
id.   id.   pour nourriture solide
Sandwiches.

Left opposite.

Free French Secret Service (BCRA), 17 June 1942. List of standard equipment for all the agents leaving in mission. On the second part are mentioned the "small" and "large" Type A, as well as a General equipment pack...
(SHD)

Opposite.

After the liberation of France. René Citerne wears the SOE jumpsuit, the Sorbo helmet and the parachute harness of Tony Brooks. His father holds the camouflaged canopy. A close look at the picture reveals that is an early type of jumpsuit (position of the three fasteners and inclusion of collar). The Sorbo helmet is much lighter in shade than those issued later in the war, which were black. The parachute is a Type A one, which was used by clandestine agents at the beginning of the war. The two hooks that were holding the parachutist's luggage between him and the canopy can easily be seen on the ground.
(Citeme, Bruno Barthelot collection)

TYPE X PARACHUTE
(TYPE X MK I RÉF. 15A/475)

Above.
Parachutist at Ringway. On this dramatic picture, it is easy to observe the 28 rigging lines gathered by seven on the four lift webs.
(IWM)

Opposite.
Tatton Park. Landing of a Polish parachutist hanging below a camouflaged Type X parachute.
(Airborne Forces Museum)

Left page, center.
Two Norwegian parachutists hanging from widely open Type X parachutes.
(Forsvarsmuseet Oslo)

Left page, opposite.
1st airborne division parachutists on 2 October 1942. Camouflaged Type X parachutes with a green harness can be seen. The facing parachutist carries a plain Quick Release Box. "D" rings can be seen on the bottom of the harness worn by the second parachutist from the right.
(IWM picture)

The Statichute or Type X parachute consists of four main elements: the canopy, the harness, the inner Pack with the static line, and the outer bag ref 15A / 475 with four flaps. The parachute provides a descent of about 22 ft per second. Its reputation of being safe is such that it was not until 1955 that the British decide to add a security parachute.

With minor modifications, the Type X remained in service with the British Army until November 1963 when it is replaced by the Type «PX», whose canopy is larger though it looks very much alike the original X Type.

Above.
A Norwegian parachutist below a Type X parachute.
(Forsvarsmuseet Oslo)

Opposite.
August 1942. Those two paratroopers belonging to the 6th Royal Welsh have just landed on Tatton Park, the Central Landing Establishment DZ near Ringway. Notice the Type X parachutes with camouflaged canopy.
(IWM)

HARNESS

Below.
Side views of the QRB from a harness used during SAS Snelgrove operation, with the manufacture number M 073932 on one side and the manufacturer's label DWCC 5 on the another.
(Collection of Emmanuel Lefebvre, picture by the author)

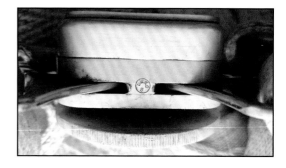

Above.
Norwegian parachutists fitting their Mk II Type X parachute before a training jump. They wear Bungey training helmets. On the parachutist bowing his head on the right of the rack, the static line can be seen on a window on the top of the outer bag with the number 4 written with a white chalk. It is easy to understand how the Oversmock is worn.
(Forsvarsmuseet Oslo)

Left opposite.
Harness used during the SAS Snelgrove operation. 28 French SAS (4th squadron of the 3d RCP/ 3d SAS BAT), divided in two sticks, jump during the night of 7 to 8 August 1944 at Fonfreyde near Bonnefonds in the Creuse departement. It is easy to follow the shape of the straps, crossing on several points before shaping four different lift webs, each bound by connector links to a set of seven suspension lines. It is a first pattern harness, with no extra fixing strap for the QRB.
(Collection of Emmanuel Lefebvre, picture by the author)

The Irvin (Smith) harness is formed by a set of straps connecting the parachutist to his parachute. 1 ¾ wide, the straps are cotton/linen with a centerline stitching colored by the manufacturer. The metal parts are nickel-plated or brushed steel. On camouflaged models, they are painted green. These straps join the right group of rigging lines to the left-wing passing under the seat of the user, forming a «U». The resistance of a single harness strap is 4500 lbs. The main U-shaped strap being composed by four single ones, its resistance rises up to 18000 lbs.

Thanks to the double cross pattern of a central strap, stitched at both ends, the harness is consolidated and adjusted to the body of the parachutist. When this strap crosses the harness, it retains two metallic lugs which will lock into the two upper hooks of the Quick Release Box Ref 15A/150 patented by Irvin in 1929.

The hardware was forged stainless steel which was latter chrome plated. The QRB has a round flat top of 3 inch diameter. An arrow and the inscription « *Turn to unlock* » and « *Press to release* » are carved on the top. It is connected to the harness through the left upper lug.

The crossing of the central strap secures the 4 flaps bag back with, where are kept the canopy, the rigging lines, the inner bag and the static line.

After the landing, the box allows the fighter to get rid virtually instantly of his parachute. The system is so effective that the US will adopt it for their T7 parachute, after many troubles with the T5. During Overlord operation especially, many American parachutists got drowned in the swamps because they could not get released quickly enough.

On the lower part of the U, next to the hips, two stitched rings are used to attach dinghy during jumps over pools.

Opposite.
1942, Norwegian paratrooper officer fitting his early-issue Mk I Type X parachute. The harness is green and the QRB unpainted.
(Forsvarsmuseet Oslo)

Norwegian parachutist fitting his Type X
parachute before a training jump. He wears
an Oversmock and a Bungey training helmet.
(Forsvarsmuseet Oslo)

Quick Release Box belonging to 3rd SAS Captain Georges Fournier

dropped during the night of 24 to 25 July 1944 at Bois d'Anjou during Dickens Operation.

Georges Fournier was born on 5 June 1909 at Rueil-Malmaison (92). Mobilized in 1939 at the 6th Colonial Infantry Regiment, he spent the winter in Wardt forest and won his first mention as head of one of the 7th cie platoons. He was mentioned a second time during the Sommauthe fights on the Somme.

Wounded by 17 shrapnel at Barizet on 20 June 1940 (3rd and 4th quotes), he was captured and incarcerated on 23 June 1940 at 17 A Offlag of Aidelbach,

Above.
Belongings of Captain George Fournier (3rd SAS battalion), dropped on 25 July 1944 from a Stirling piloted by Squadron Leader Angell (196 sqd) during the Dickens operation. The DZ was located near the farm of Chantegrolle, West of Bois d'Anjou, in the Maine et Loire department. From top to bottom: his personal flag, his maroon beret, his Battle dress with Free French Paratroops wings and SAS wings, as well as his medals: Légion d'Honneur, 39-45 War Cross with five mentions, including two palms, and the Military Cross. The Quick Release Box is part of the Type X parachute he used during this mission.
(Collection of Emmanuel Lefebvre, picture by the author)

Below.
Front view of Captain Georges Fournier's QRB. Three harness lugs can be unlocked by turning the plate clockwise before smartly hitting it.
(Collection of Emmanuel Lefebvre, picture by the author)

Above.
Captain Georges Fournier in 1945, wearing the blue French Airforces uniform decorated with the Free France parachutist wings and his three main medals: Légion d'Honneur, War cross with five mentions, including two palms and the Military Cross.
(Collection of Emmanuel Lefebvre)

Opposite.
**Side view of Captain Fournier's QRB with manufacture number M 133515.
Side view of the opposite side of Captain Fournier's QRB, with AML 5 manufacturer's label.**
(Collection of Emmanuel Lefebvre, picture by the author)

in Austria. After feigning being deaf for 5 months, he was repatriated for sanitary reasons on 20 March 1941. As soon as he was back in France, Georges Fournier applied for a post in Vichy army in Indochina, hoping that he would find a way to gain London when crossing along Gibraltar. He left France on 4 May 1941, but his plan of escape failed and he landed at Haiphong on 1 August 1941. He was assigned to the 3rd Rifle Tonkinese Regiment then to the 9th RIC and to the 4th RTT. One evening of March 1943, he took his chance during an inspection tour and with two other comrades he gained by bike Nationalist China. At Tchoung-King he signs his act of recruitment on Free French Forces. After a long sailing by Calcutta and Bombay, he reached Middle East and then Alexandria. On 2 July 1943 he met the commander Bourgoin «the Penguin» who invited him to join the paratrooper battalion he was creating. On 15 July 1943 he took command of the paratrooper detachment at Rayack and gained Cairo on 15 August 1943. He was directed to Camberley in England where he arrived on 11 November 1943 to be appointed deputy to Captain Château-Jobert of the 3d SAS. He started his SAS training, was qualified as Free French parachutist on 6 January 1944, and granted certificate number 3003.

Georges Fournier took command of the 3rd Squadron of Auchinleck camp.

He was dropped during the night of 24 to 25 July 1944 at Bois d'Anjou during Dickens Operation. On 27 September 1944, Georges Fournier was shot again on his shoulder, near the mill of Frossey, south of Saint-Nazaire. He was granted his 5th mention. Assigned to DGER on 21 December 1944, he was responsible for preparing an SAS operation on Berlin which finally didn't take place.

Promoted to the rank of Commandant on 25 December 1944, he was granted the Military Cross with on mention on 5 March 1945. He spent the end of the war as special Adviser to the Nazi war criminals research unit from 7 May 1945 to 1 July 1948. He left army for civilian life as agricultural engineer.

Officer of the Legion d'Honneur, with 6 mentions, he was wounded twice. He died on 7 December 1996 at Beaulieu-sur-Mer (Alpes Maritimes).

INNER BAG AND STATIC LINE

The bag contains the canopy and allows stowing the rigging lines on one of the flaps. Manufactured in a durable cloth, it is rectangular in shape and opens at one side. When the canopy is packed inside, four cloth flaps are folded to keep it apart from the rigging lines. On one of the flaps of the size of the bag, the suspension lines are stowed under ten bungee cords (elastic loops) that are kept together until they open in four groups of seven at the end of the lift webs.

At the other end of the bag, the 12 ft static line is sewn on strong reinforcements made from the same type of cotton braided straps 1 ¾ wide. The static line is double thick. It passes into the inner bag. Its end is connected by a 110 lb break cord tie surrounding all the rigging lines at the top of the packed canopy. The tie is made with some stowed and sewn rigging lines. It has the same color than they have and it is camouflaged when the canopy is camouflaged.

During the opening sequence, the static line gets fully uncoiled, then the rigging lines, the canopy stretches and the string of the tie breaks at the maximum tension. The tie remains at the top of the canopy. After the landing, parachutists are used to keep the tie as a souvenir or to use it as a strap with small objects like watches, compasses or penknives.

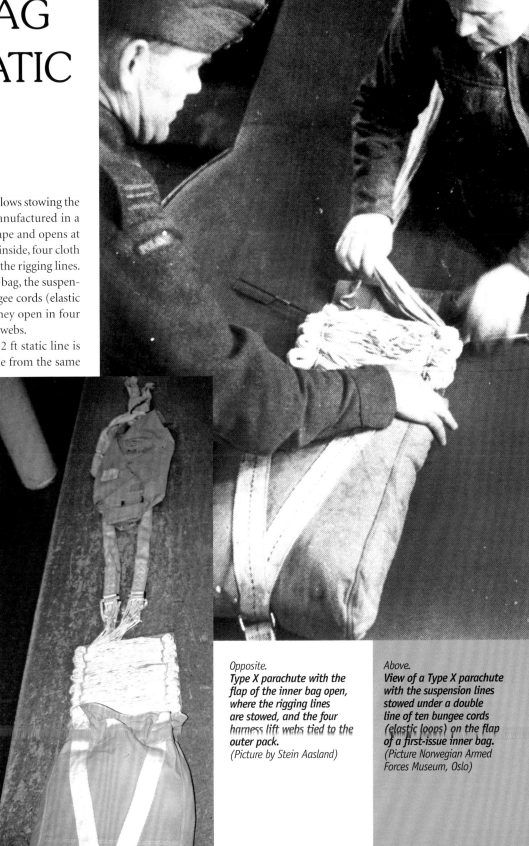

Opposite.
Type X parachute with the flap of the inner bag open, where the rigging lines are stowed, and the four harness lift webs tied to the outer pack.
(Picture by Stein Aasland)

Above.
View of a Type X parachute with the suspension lines stowed under a double line of ten bungee cords (elastic loops) on the flap of a first-issue inner bag.
(Picture Norwegian Armed Forces Museum, Oslo)

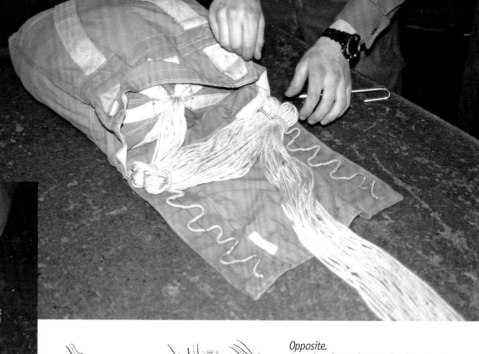

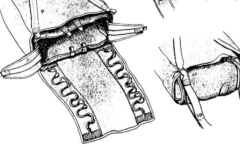

Opposite.
Drawing from the regular handbook showing the specificities of the first type outer pack, including the flap of the inner bag with the double line of bungee cords.
(Airborne Forces Museum)

Below.
Another tie of a Type X used as a handle for a British regular clock.
(Musée de la Résistance bretonne at Saint Marcel)

Opposite.
Type X parachute tie used by a French parachutist of the 4th SAS Battalion as a wrist strap for the handle of a Jack Knife.
(Musée de la Résistance bretonne at Saint Marcel)

Below.
White tie of the parachute of Lieutenant Alain Calloc'h de Kerillis. De Kerillis, a.k.a. Richard Skinner (radio code Pierre 411) was dropped in Brittany during the SAS Cooney Parties, 7 June 1944. His mission was to destroy the railway between Vannes and Questembert. Wounded and arrested on 14 July 1944, he was tortured and executed on 18 July 1944 at Rimaison.
(Collection and picture by the author)

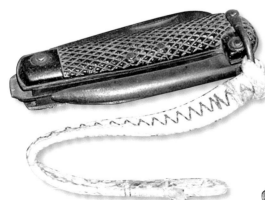

The camouflaged tie of Achille Muller

(4th SAS, jumps on 23 October 1943)

Achille Muller leaves Forbach on 14 July 1942 and crosses four boarders: the Franco-German one (since Lorraine is annexed), demarcation line, the boarder with Spain and eventually the line between Gibraltar and Spain.

Arrived in England on 4 March 1943, he volunteers to serve in the parachutists of the France Combattante in the 4th SAS (2d RCP). He is qualified as a parachutist at Ringway on 23 June 1943 with patent number 21299.

At the end of July 1943, Lieutenant Pierre Marienne, head of the 2d section of the 1st cie of SAS 4th BAT, receives the mission to leave for the Airborne experimental establishment located on a RAF base at Sheburn (Helmet) to take part to special tests.

From mi-September to early December 1943, Section is on training, studying and rehearsing every jumps technics from various aircraft (Dakota, Stirling, Albermale et Halifax) and even from a Horsa glider. New materials are tried and tested (canopy, static lines, etc). The training is difficult, often risky but exciting. For the first time, the French parachutists are granted the means that they lacked. Marienne Section never gets enough and always volunteers to further tries. On 23 October 1943, the section breaks a world record. Twenty SAS jump from a C 47 Dakota in 7 seconds and 5/10' in less than 425 yards. A very risky exercise since the issue can often turn lethal if two parachutists get entangled with no security parachute.

On this very day, Achille Muller is the 13th man to jump. He decides to keep the tie of his parachute for good luck. One still can see that it is a camouflaged tie, which means that his canopy on the world record jump was camouflaged too.

Achille Muller is then trained as a jeep driver. He is landed by glider on the evening of 5 August 1944 at Ederven near Locoal-Mendon during SAS Dingson operation.

Driving his jeep he takes part to the infiltrating manoeuvre on the South of the Loire to harass the enemy and provide intelligence to the Allies (Spencer operation).

Above.
Private Achille Muller in August 1943.
(Collection of Achille Muller)

Back at Ipswitch, in South-East England, he is dropped on 7 April 1945 near Schoonloo in Holland during Amherst operation.

Promoted to the rank of officer, Achille Muller becomes a career parachutist, continuing his service in Indochina and in Algeria.

Colonel Achille Muller is grand officier de la légion d'honneur with 8 mentions, including 3 palms.

Opposite.
Airbone Pegasus and tie of the Type X parachute Achille Muller (SAS 4th Bat, Marienne Platoon) used for his world record jump from a Dakota on 23 October 1943. This camouflaged tie is a positive clue that Achille on that very day jumped with a camouflaged Type X!
(Collection of Emmanuel Lefebvre, picture by the author)

43

Above.
This parachutist is checking that his static line is properly attached to the 9'9" strobe used in the C 47 Dakota as low anchor line cable .
(IWM)

The parachutist is no more connected to the dropping plane. Once the canopy is fully extracted from its bag, it takes its fully swollen shape. The other end of the static line, intended to be fixed on the plane, ends in V-ring snaps. The static V-rings are snapped onto a web extension called a strop, which is itself connected by a D-ring to the anchor line cable. The strop varies in length depending on the dropping airplanes, Abermarle, Halifax or C 47 Dakota. On Whitley and Wellington, their length can also vary according to the place of the parachutist among the jumpers' line, for the plane's center of gravity moves after each jump. On the Wellington, the Whitley, the Abermarle and the Halifax, 10 parachutists can be carried. On the Whitley, they seat five by five on each side of the jumping pit. On a Wellington, six have to seat on the front and 4 at the back. In a Halifax, it has to be 8 on the front and 2 at the back. Only on the Abermarle can the 10 parachutists stand on the same line.

Eventually, the length of the extensions is different according to the type of dropping plane: 6" on the Abermarle, 16' on the Halifax and 9'9" on the C 47 Dakota.

Recordmen in jumping order:

1- LTN Pierre Marienne
2- ADJ Auguste Chilou
3- 1CL Clément Goder
4- 1CL Pierre Hoareau
5- 1CL Emmanuel Ismar
6- 1CL Alexandre Le Maou
7- 1CL Charles Schweitzer
8- CPL Claude Fraise
9- SAS Alain Le Corre
10- CPL Gérard Racine

11- CPL Émile Bouétard
12- CL Alexandre de Alma
13- CL Achille Muller
14- CL Michel Lakermance
15- CL Jean Soldevilla
16- CL André Vernet
17- CL Louis Le Floch
18- CCH Antoine Treis
19- SCH Loïc Raufast
20- ASP Georges Taylor

Below.
Marienne platoon surrounding the crew that dropped them from a Dakota on 23 October 1943.
(Collection of Achille Muller)

Opposite.
Parachutistes emplaning into a C 47 Dakota. They are equipped with a Mk II Type X with no external pockets for the static line.
(Collection Jean-François Lemoine)

Below.
Rear view of a Mk I Type X parachute with the two vertical external pockets where the static line is stowed.
(Collection Jean-François Lemoine)

Opposite.
Checking of the holding of the static line to the 9'9" strobe used for the C 47 Dakota. The parachutist wearing motorbike gloves is equipped with a Kit bag.
(IWM)

Below.
The static lines of these British parachutists are hanged to big strobes for high anchor line cable. A careful observer may notice that their harness have no rings for chest parachutes, which means that they can be dated before 1955.
(Airborne Forces Museum)

Pack Outer

The pack outer is on the back of the parachutist. The bottom comprises a rectangular half-rigid base of 25,5 cm x 46,5cm whose four flaps close to keep the canopy bag inside. The four flaps are provided with grommets or buckets; they are kept tied together by a 55 lb breaking tie. A set of three lugs are closed by « LIFT THE DOT » pressure buttons. Placed in Y, they keep the pack connected to the harness straps. Like the canopy it contains, it can be beige colored or camouflaged. Usually camouflaged canopies are found with camouflaged packs. The pack contains part of the static line, the canopy in its bag, the rigging lines and the upper part of the lift webs. The static line is stowed vertically outside the pack in two small fabric pockets of 5 x 2 x 1'4".

Below from left to right.
Mk I Type X outer pack with the static line stowed in two external pockets of 5x2x1'4".

Back of a Mk I Type X outer pack with the three recognizable harness straps shaping a Y. Inside view of a Mk I Type X outer pack. The reinforcement is made of a 10 x 18 ¼" fiber plate set on the sewn lining.
(Picture by and collection of Charly Roussel)

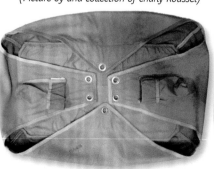

General appearance and dating

On the very first pictures of 1940-1941, the parachutes are shown with a white, green or brown dark colored harness and pack outer. The metallic pieces, QRB and setting rings, are nickel plated-shiny. Canopy, rigging lines and tie are camouflaged.

Special Services favor the Type A, then the camouflaged version of the Type X, whose buckles set can be painted green. A black canopy version is generally granted as specific SOE. In 1944 tactical light brown or white canopies can be used on special missions.

Later on, the Mk I types X are produced with a khaki-beige pack outer and a white harness with brush steel buckles. On some pictures as well, the harness is green and the pack outer is khaki-beige colored.

Above.
British paratroopers emplaning into a Whitley at The Central landing Establishment in Ringway. Notice the Mk I Type X parachutes.
(IWM)

Opposite.
1942, Norwegian paratroopers drawing their early Mk I Type X. The static line is stowed outside the dark outer pack and the harness is green. The men wear parachutist jackets.
(Forsvarsmuseet Oslo)

Left page.
A parachutist is helping a fellow to lock the harness of his Mk I Type X. They wear early-issue equipments: dark outer pack, parachutist jacket and Bungey training helmet.
(Airborne Forces Museum)

Opposite.
Parachute trainees boarding an aircraft in Ringway under the watchful eyes of an RAF Dispatcher.
They wear Mk I Type X parachutes, where the Static line is stowed in two external pockets.
(Airborne Forces Museum)

Above.
A 1ˢᵗ Airborne division stick about to emplane into a Whitley in October 1942.
(IWM)

Left page.
Four 1ˢᵗ Airborne division paratroopers being photographed on 2 October 1942. They are equipped with camouflaged Mk I Type X. The D rings are easy to see, as well as the unpainted QRB and the beige-khaki inner bags.
(IWM)

Opposite.
Side view of two British paratroopers equipped with camouflaged Mk I Type X parachutes. Their harness is white with three stitching lines, a quite rare design.
(IWM)

Below.
The tie of the camouflaged Type X parachutes is manufactured with a piece of camouflaged rigging line.
(Collection and pictures of the author)

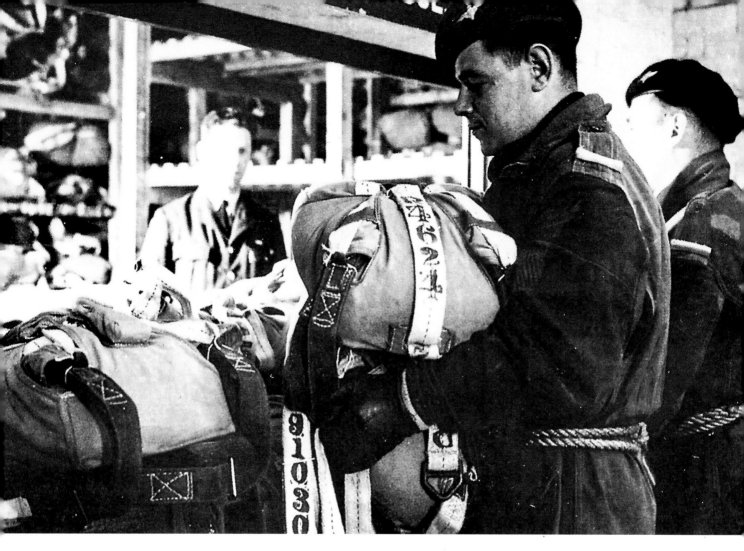

Above.
British paratroopers receiving their parachutes in a store. The first one carries in his arms a Mk II Type X with a green harness while a Mk I with a green harness is also placed on the bank in front of him.
(IWM)

Opposite.
British paratroopers wearing Type X parachutes with a green or a white harness.
(IWM)

Next page, from top to bottom.
1942, Norwegian paratrooper officer fitting his early-issue Mk I Type X Mk I parachute. The harness is green and the QRB unpainted.
(Airborne Forces Museum)

1942, stick of Norwegian paratroopers emplaning into a Whitley. Notice the Parachutists jackets and the early-issued Mk I Type X parachute. The static line is stowed outside, the harness is green and the outer bag camouflaged. But the load rings of the harness are square and the QRB is not painted in green.
(Forsvarsmuseet Oslo)

Opposite.
Rear view of a Mk I Type X parachute. The white harness has a black central line stitching. The QRB is marked with number M 96570 on one side and AML 5 manufacture mark on the other one.
(Collection of and picture by Laurent Jacquet)

Above.
Parachutiste with a camouflaged Type X canopy at Tatton Park.
(Airborne Forces Museum)

Opposite..
Front view of a Mk I Type X parachute. The white harness has a black central line stitching.
(Collection of and picture by Laurent Jacquet)

Opposite.
On 13 July 1943, 1st brigade paratroopers putting on camouflaged Mk I Type X on a Tunisia airfield. Their aim is Primosole bridge on Simeto River, South of Catania in Sicily. The D rings are easy to observe, as well as the unpainted QRB and the beige-khaki inner bags.
(IWM)

Below.
Side view of the green-painted QRB (M 75843) of a camouflaged Mk I Type X parachute found in France.
Opposite side of the green-painted QRB with its AML 5 manufacture mark of a camouflaged Mk I Type X parachute found in France.
(Private collection, picture by the author)

Above.
Green-painted QRB of a camouflaged Mk I Type X parachute found in France.
(Private collection, picture by the author)

Below, from left to right.
Early production Mk I Type X with a green harness, green painted buckles, and a camouflaged outer pack.
(Private collection, picture by the author)

Mk I Type X outer pack connected to the harness thanks to three straps shaping a Y.
(Picture by the author, private collection)

Opposite.
Mannequin with the equipment of Ernest Henry Van Maurik, dropped from a Squadron 138 Halifax during "Marksman 13" operation, on the night of 7 to 8 January 1944, over DZ Izemore, 4 miles North-East of Nantua (Ain). The black canopy he is holding comes from a container parachute.
(Musée de la Résistance et de la Déportation of Nantua, picture by the author)

Above.
Ernest Henry Van Maurik a.k.a. Patterson, was dropped over Izemore DZ during the night of January, 7 to 8, 1944. After spending ten days or so inspecting the Ain maquis, "Patterson" was smuggled to Switzerland thanks to Resistants of Combat movement. He then took the head of the SOE legation in Berne in April 1944.
(Musée de la Résistance et de la Déportation of Nantua)

Below.
On Ernest Henry Van Maurik's parachute, the harness is green and the QRB unpainted.
(Musée de la Résistance et de la Déportation of Nantua, picture by the author)

A British staff sergeant is about to jump from a C 47 Dakota. The khaki-beige outer pack of his Type X parachute is coupled to a green harness. (IWM)

TYPE X MK I MODIFIED 15A/495

This modified version of Mk I pack outer has kept the two external pockets where the static line is stowed, but it already has the four fixing loops closed by "lift the door" snaps shaping an X in the back. It has the reference 15A/495.

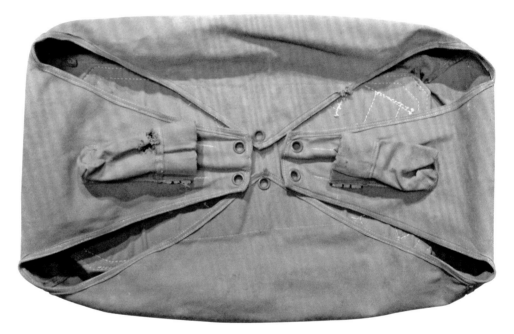

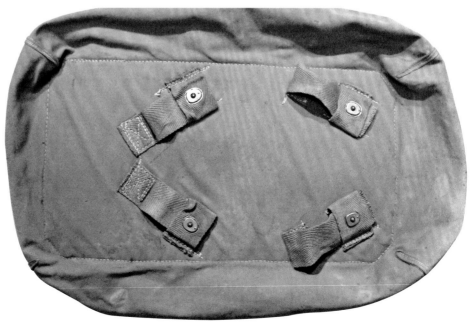

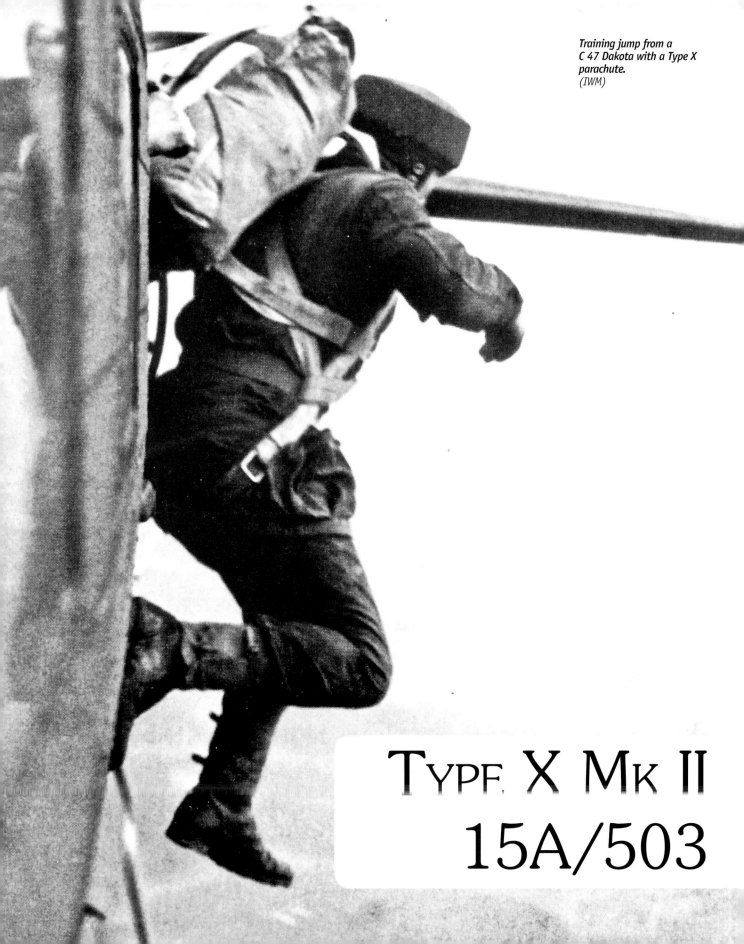

Training jump from a
C 47 Dakota with a Type X
parachute.
(IWM)

Type X Mk II
15A/503

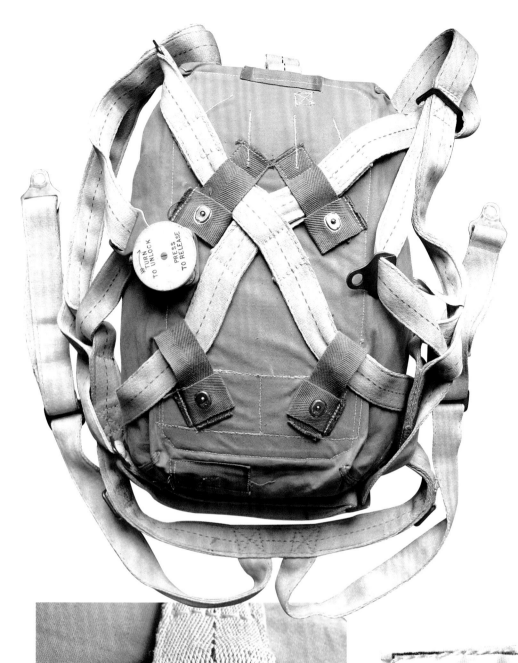

Opposite
Inner side of the outer pack of a Mk II Type X parachute found in the South-East of France. The four harness straps shaping a X are very easy to observe.
(Collection of and picture by the author)

Below, from left to right.
Close up on the slot of the Mk II Type X outer pack. The static line is better protected by being stowed directly inside the outer pack.

Label sewn on the outside of the outer pack of a Mk II Type X parachute found in the South-East of France. BP OUTER PACK MkII REF N°15A/503 and red ink stamp 17 August xx 6157.
(Collection of and picture by the author)

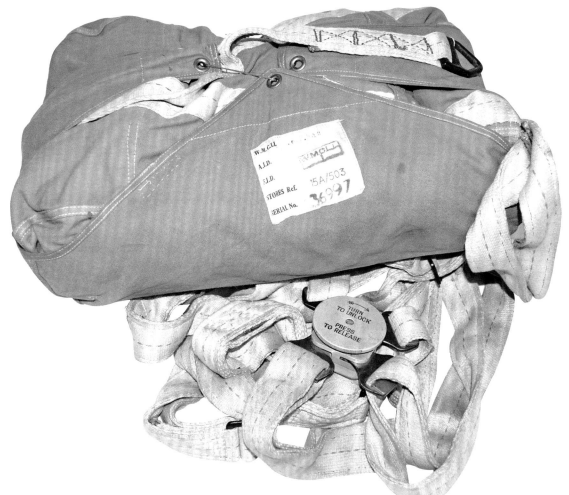

Modifications with the outer pack, the QRB, the inner bag and the stowage of the static line

To increase the safety and efficiency without having to change the general pattern, some changes are made on Pack Outer ref 15/503 and on the inner bag. The positioning of the static line is changed as well as its stowing and that of the rigging lines. The canopy is protected by an inner sock and the rigging lines are now stowed over two parallel stowing lines sewn to the external side of the pack outer.

With this new system, the static line is positioned again in the pack outer. It's now stowed vertically inside, between the inner pack and the bottom of the pack. It passes through the static extraction slot provided on the top flap to stow in four inner canvas loops. The external pockets of the outer pack where the static line was stowed are suppressed.

The parachute, packed this way, is ready for use. During the jump, the static line is regularly and vertically deployed on a controlled way, so as to reduce the risks of dangerous twists in operational low-altitude drops.

A strap is added on the left side of the harness to hold the QRB permanently. The added strap passes through a slot on a plate screwed to the back of the QRB. Except for the QRB, all the buckles are painted black.

The harness of the war Mk II Type X is colored white. The design and color (blue, orange, red and black, black) of the center line stitching are manufacturing codes.

Above.
Mk II Type X parachute recovered in Norway. The two vertical pockets used to stowe the static line outside the bag have been replaced by a slot on top of the bag.
(Forsvarsmuseet Oslo)

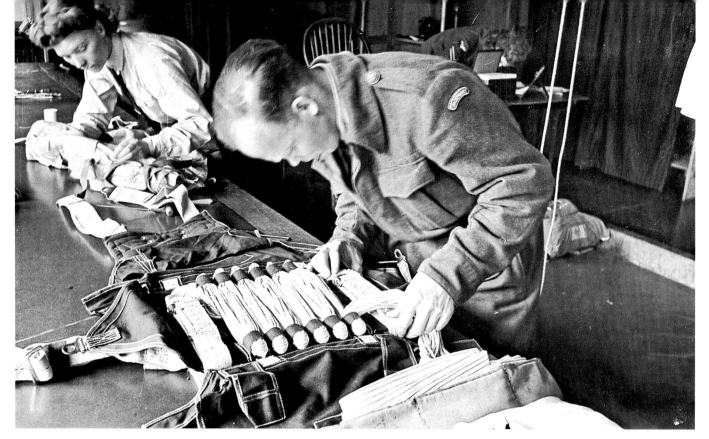

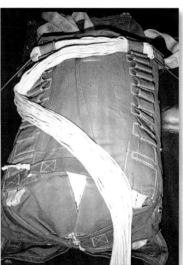

Above.
Rigging lines must be stowed with great care and regularity.
(Forsvarsmuseet Oslo)

Opposite.
Close up on the parallel canvas stowing lines of the 2d type of inner bag, with the Newey snaps on the side of the pack.
(Stein Aasland)

Below, from left to right.
Label "TYPE "X"/ "KMK"" and "15A/503" sewn on the Mk II Type X outer pack from the Cooney parties.

Label "TYPE "X KMK" and "15A/429" sewn on the Mk II Type X outer pack from the Cooney parties.
(Collection Emmanuel Lefebvre)

Right page.
A Norwegian soldier is finishing to stowe the rigging lines of a Type X parachute.
(Forsvarsmuseet Oslo)

Next page at the bottom right.
Drawing from the regular handbook showing the specificities of the 2d type of inner bag. The flap is now covering two parallel canvas stowing lines allowing to stowe the rigging lines. Since 1956, the flap is kept closed by two Newey snaps.
(Airborne Forces Museum)

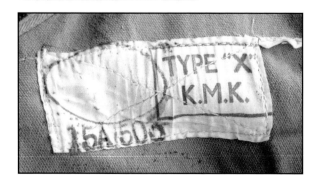

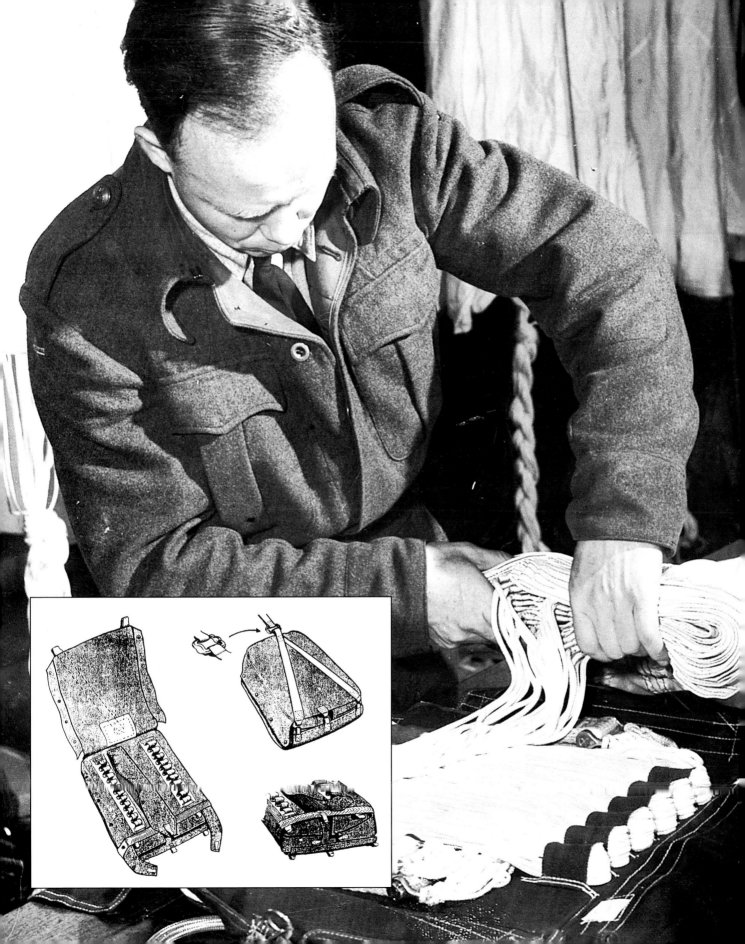

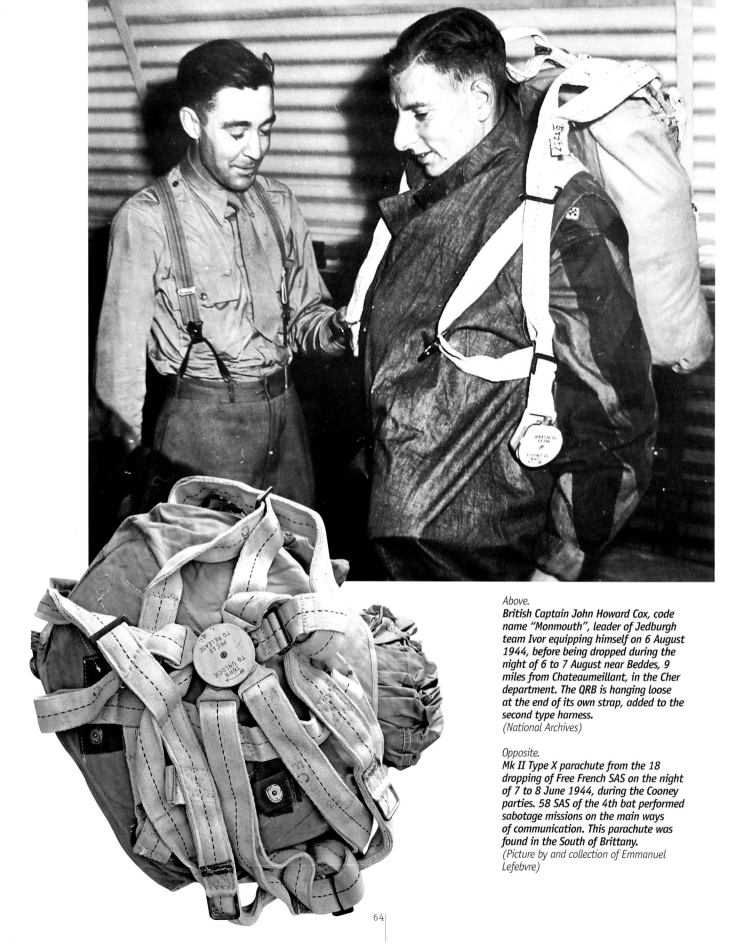

Above.

British Captain John Howard Cox, code name "Monmouth", leader of Jedburgh team Ivor equipping himself on 6 August 1944, before being dropped during the night of 6 to 7 August near Beddes, 9 miles from Chateaumeillant, in the Cher department. The QRB is hanging loose at the end of its own strap, added to the second type harness.
(National Archives)

Opposite.

Mk II Type X parachute from the 18 dropping of Free French SAS on the night of 7 to 8 June 1944, during the Cooney parties. 58 SAS of the 4th bat performed sabotage missions on the main ways of communication. This parachute was found in the South of Brittany.
(Picture by and collection of Emmanuel Lefebvre)

Below.
Label "TYPE "X"" and "15A/381" sewn on the Mk II Type X outer pack from the Cooney parties.
(Picture by and collection of Emmanuel Lefebvre)

Below.
Side views of the QRB (M 155934) of a Mk II Type X from the Cooney parties, with its DWCC II manufacture mark.
(Picture by and collection of Emmanuel Lefebvre)

Opposite.
Harness of the second type with a QRB on a strap. This harness belonged to OSS operational group (OG) Christopher, dropped over DZ Anicroche, 0,6 mile East of Salives in Côte d'Or, on 4 September 1944 at 1' 30", during the "Bob 172" operation. Led by US Captain Melvin J. Hjeltness, 54 OSS paratroopers jumped from ten B 24, followed by a 11th plane exclusively loaded with containers to be dropped on the very same night. 120 in all will be found on the ground.
(Picture by and collection of Charly Roussel)

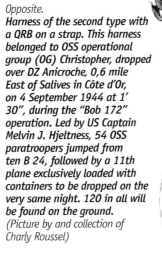

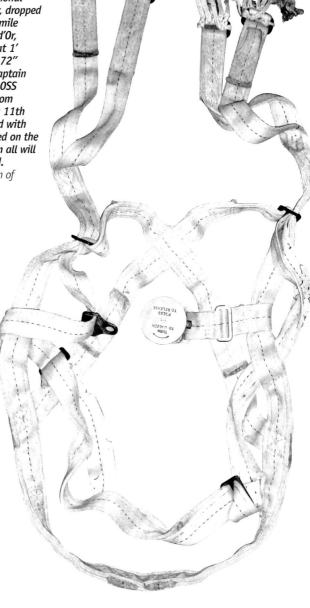

Below.
Front view of a QRB with the strap of a 2d type harness. The metal plate added to the back of the box is a 2,36 inch large square. Opposite side of the OG Christopher QRB with its AML 5 manufacture mark.
(Collection Charly Roussel)

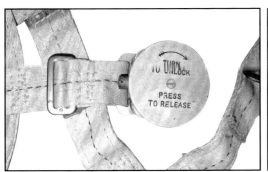

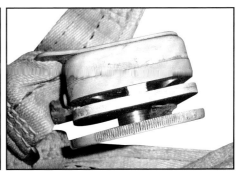

White type X intended for Northern countries Equipement

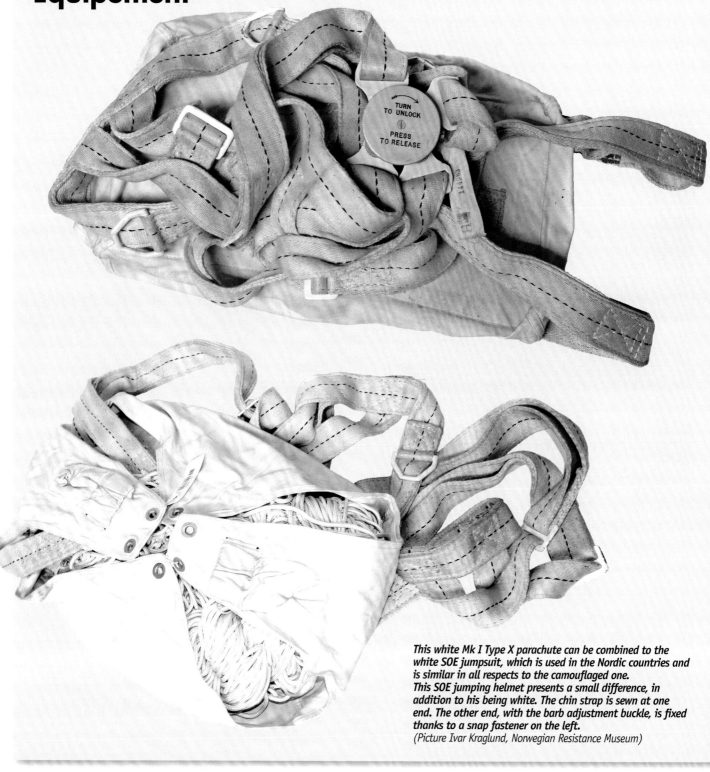

This white Mk I Type X parachute can be combined to the white SOE jumpsuit, which is used in the Nordic countries and is similar in all respects to the camouflaged one.
This SOE jumping helmet presents a small difference, in addition to his being white. The chin strap is sewn at one end. The other end, with the barb adjustment buckle, is fixed thanks to a snap fastener on the left.
(Picture Ivar Kraglund, Norwegian Resistance Museum)

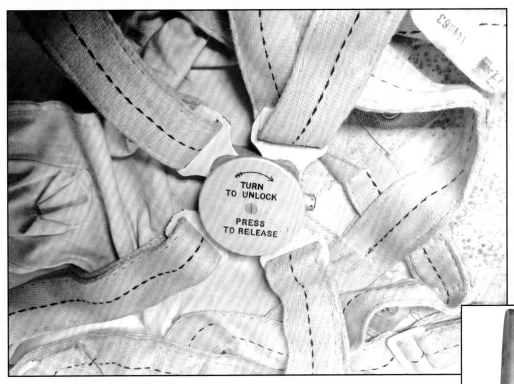

TURN
TO UNLOCK

PRESS
TO RELEASE

Opposite.
On the harness, a fabric label is marked with the inscription H 144963. The QRB is a first version one and has no fixing strap.
(Picture Ivar Kraglund, Norwegian Resistance Museum)

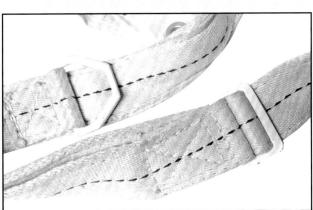

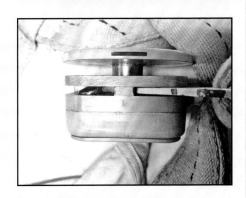

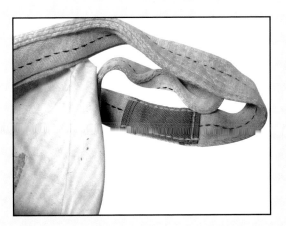

Opposite, from top to bottom.
White Mk I Type X. All the buckles are painted in white as well.

The famous rectangular label of the harness is made out of a brown fabric
(Picture Ivar Kraglund, Norwegian Resistance Museum)

Above, from top to bottom.
The registration number of the QRB is M 58649.

On the opposite side of the QRB, the manufacturer's label AML 5 can be seen.
(Picture Ivar Kraglund, Norwegian Resistance Museum)

Left opposite.
Side view of the same exhibition, allowing to see the harness of the Type A on the mannequin equipped with the white SOE jumpsuit known as the « Norwegian trooper's ».
(National Archives)

Ci-contre à droite.
Close up on the « Norwegian trooper » equipped with a Type A. A special attention has to be given to the hooks connecting the lift webs and their extension line, as well as to the large size of the supplies pack at the feet of the mannequin.
(National Archives)

Below.
STS 15 b. All the SOE equipment of the STS 15 Station are displayed in exhibition at the Natural History Museum of London. Under the sign "JO's equipment" surmounted by the royal crown, are presented the pieces of equipment of the agents dropped on occupied Europe. The atmosphere is given by a brick wall where one can watched the inscription "A bas sales Boches" ("Down with the Boche"), the drawing of a hanged man and a German poster of the Feldkommandant. On the left, a mannequin equipped with a white jumpsuit is hanging with a Type A harness.

The hooks connected to the lift webs extension lines can be neatly seen. The supplies pack at its feet should have been displayed fixed to the harness by the same hooks. The scene is completed by two containers, the second one being covered with a tree trunk camouflage canvas, a Kit bag and a second hanging mannequin, equipped with a camouflaged jumpsuit and SOE overshoes. On both case, the QRB is not painted in green.
(National Archives)

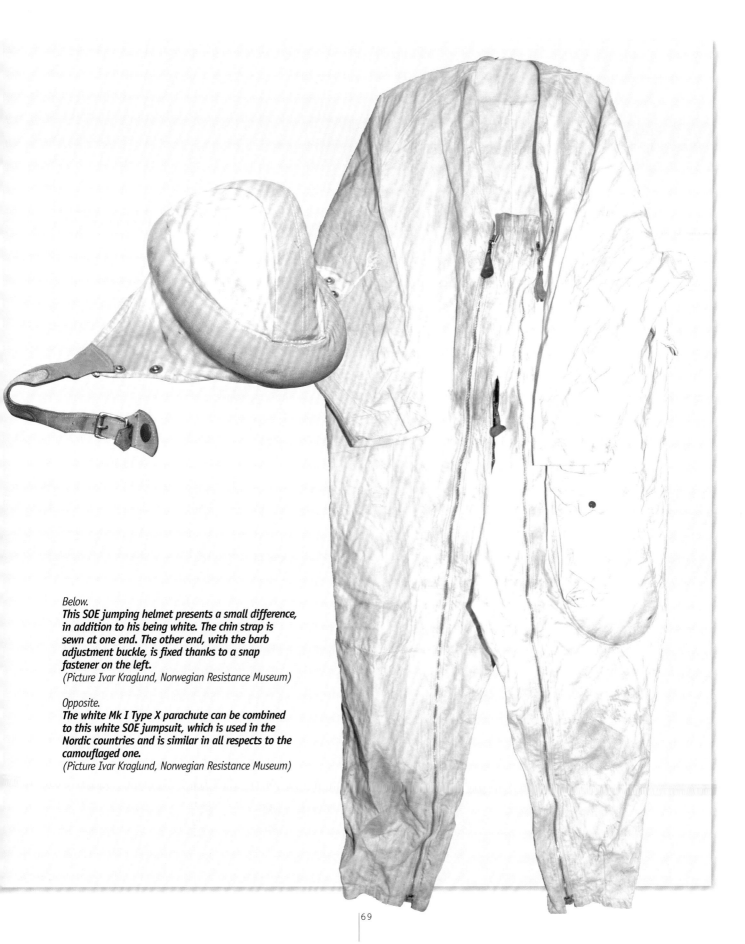

Below.
This SOE jumping helmet presents a small difference, in addition to his being white. The chin strap is sewn at one end. The other end, with the barb adjustment buckle, is fixed thanks to a snap fastener on the left.
(Picture Ivar Kraglund, Norwegian Resistance Museum)

Opposite.
The white Mk I Type X parachute can be combined to this white SOE jumpsuit, which is used in the Nordic countries and is similar in all respects to the camouflaged one.
(Picture Ivar Kraglund, Norwegian Resistance Museum)

EQUIPMENT

Once loaded, the container is brought to the Whitley.
(Forsvarsmuseet Oslo)

Opposite.
British paratrooper posing with a Mk I Type X and a Kit bag. It is open on one end, and down one side the entire aperture is fitted with brass grommets and laced with cord. On the left side, the 20 ft suspension lines are stowed inside a canvas pocket. It is an early-issue parachute with legs straps in leather but no anti-sear sleeve nor Jettison device.
(Airborne Force Experimental Establishment Ministry of Supply)

Opposite.
The sergeant armed with a Mk II Sten gun is protecting the men unpacking the light machine guns. The felt dust covers precede the Bren valise and the Rifle valise.
(IWM)

The photographs of the beginning of the war reveal that the British followed the example of the Russian and German precursors, and took the option to cast individual and collectives weapons, as well as heavy equipment, in containers dropped in the same time than the parachutists. This method quickly reveals a major drawback: the slightest dropping delay leaves the parachutists on the ground deprived from any fire support. The problem becomes more acute when it is decided that the dropping will take place by night. In the dark, these supplies containers are even more difficult to find and collect. To solve the problem, the British imitate the system used by the French parachutists as early as 1935 and develop two attached equipment: the "leg Kit bag" and the "light machine gun (LMG) valise". Fixed to the right side of the harness, they improve significantly the carrying capacity. The first tests are performed with leather attached equipments which allow to bind automatic pistols, Sten Gun or rifles to the parachutist's leg.

The main idea is that the attached equipment remains closely tied to the body of the parachutist during the jumping and the parachute's opening sequence. Once the parachute is properly open, the parachutist can let the attached equipment go loose thanks to a quick release system. The load is suspended beneath the parachutist thanks to a suspension line 20 ft long. During night jumps, when the attached equipment hits the ground 20 ft before the parachutist, the noise and the loosing of the tension of the line give him a precious indication that his landing is soon to happen, since he has no other clues.

The system is approved of and several kinds of attached equipment are produced.

Opposite.
View from the back of a paratrooper with a Kit bag. Two web straps keep his Kit bag secured tight to his right leg. It is a later pattern with web leg straps, an anti-sear sleeve and a Jettison device.
(Airborne Force Experimental Establishment Ministry of Supply)

Above.
Norwegian paratroopers at the end of their training session at Ringway, loading their supplies container. At the beginning of the war, the British took the option to drop rifles and light machine guns, as well as heavy equipment, in containers dropped with the parachutists. This method quickly reveals a major drawback: the slightest dropping delay leaves the parachutists on the ground deprived from any fire support.
(Forsvarsmuseet Oslo)

Opposite.
Poster reminding the main precautions to be taken with the fighting equipment on board of the plane, including the Kit bag and the Bren valise.
(Airborne Forces Museum)

Prepare for Action

① HOOK UP STATIC LINE TO STROP
② SECURE KIT-BAG LEG STRAPS
③ ATTACH KIT-BAG JETTISON DEVICE
④ ATTACH VALISE LEG STRAP
⑤ ATTACH VALISE NECK BAND

AIRBORNE FORCES PARACHUTE TRAINING

FITTING EQUIPMENT IN AIRCRAFT

4855

Above.
A less than orthodox exit from a Whitley. It is possible to
see on that picture containers parachuted on the same time
than men, containing individual and heavy weapons.
(IWM)

Opposite.
King George reviewing the 22nd Independant Parachute
Company of the 6th Airborne Division Pathfinders. They will
be the first ones to jump on the night of 5 to 6 June 1944.
(IWM)

Just landed, this parachutist is busy trying to open the Mk III CLE container to access the rifles and light machine guns.
(IWM)

EXPERIMENTAL STEN VALISE

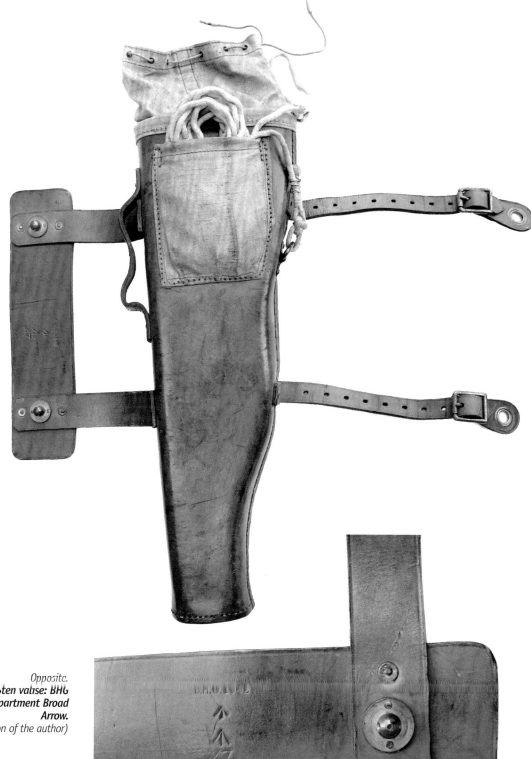

Opposite.
Sten valise, already meant to be tied to the parachutist's leg by a « pin and cone » release system. The valise was set loose in air to hang at the end of the suspension line. The Kit bag will be designed on the same system.

Opposite.
Marks stamped on the Sten valise: BHG 1942 and British War Department Broad Arrow.
(Picture by and collection of the author)

58

1.7

Commande d'ouverture du
parachute

parachute dorsal

parachute ventral

sac à vivres

harnais du parachute

parachute (4 chargeurs)

sac aux accessoires et béquille

Opposite.
Left side view of a French Air Infantryman in the 1936 pattern. In addition to the main back pack and the chest pack, the parachutist carries on his left side a valise for supplies and crutch, as well as an ammunition pouch comprising four light machine gun magazines. The haversack is visible under the chest pack.
(National Paratroopers Museum, Pau)

Opposite.

Air Festival, 10 July 1938 at Villacoublay. The Air Infantry troopers' units are introduced to the President before 250 000 spectators. On this picture, several valises for long guns secured on the left thigh can be noticed, as well as chest haversacks and one leather satchel.
(National Paratroopers Museum, Pau)

Below, from left to right.

France, 1936. The pilot Alfred Horvatte, parachutist monitor, is posing equipped with a back pack-chest pack set, a canvas gun valise on his right side and a food haversack under his chest pack. Alfred Horvatte is a veteran from the Riff fightings in Morocco. Having volunteered in Air Forces, he is granted his flying license on 25 March 1929 (certificate n° 22570). In 1935, he volunteers to jump in parachute and joins the Parachute Instruction Center at Avignon-Pujaut, where he receives patent n°4 of parachute instructor. Taught by his experience of fighting, he elaborates the operational use of parachutists and experiences several jumps carrying weapons. In three year time, he jumps 47 times before volunteering to lead an Air fighter squadron in Indochina. Lieutenant-colonel Alfred Horvatte jumps for the last time at the age of 85. He dies on 17 June 1996.

Air infantryman in jumpsuit. A canvas valise, fixed to his belt and to his leg by a leather strap, is meant to contain his weapon whose butt is protected by its own pad. It is easy to observe the 26 ft long metallic cable intended for the dropping and stowed in a canvas horizontal pocket. The operational equipment also contains a food haversack at the level of the stomach. This system is invented in 1936 when Captain Geille is appointed to prepare the setting up of the first paratroopers units. The first landing tests demonstrate how uncomfortable it is to land with a long gun at the hand or even worse along the leg. The solution chosen is to wait until the canopy is properly open, then to unhook the belt 55 yards or so before the ground. The whole bundle gun/ammunition/food goes loose and ends up hanging at the end of the steel cable suspension line attached to the harness of the parachute. Such a solution foreshadows the Kit bag system.
(National Paratroopers Museum, Pau)

LEG KIT BAG

Introduced in 1943, its official naming is Leg Kit Bag but it's more often referred to as the Leg bag or the Kit bag. It is shaped as a duffle bag, 30" high and 14½" round. It is manufactured in a strong canvas of khaki or green cotton and is intended for a maximum load of 60 lb. It can resist individual equipment and short guns, like Sten guns or USM1 A1 carbine. But its loading is up to each parachutist, and the overloaded Kit bag often happens to fall, causing the loss of the guns and equipment.

It is open on one end and down one side the entire aperture is fitted with brass grommets and laced with cords. Designed to be worn on the right leg, the Kit bag has a 4 inch thick resilient base. A slot in base allows the passage of the foot of the parachutist.

Two Special Quick release leather straps, that will become web straps in later patterns, are connected to a

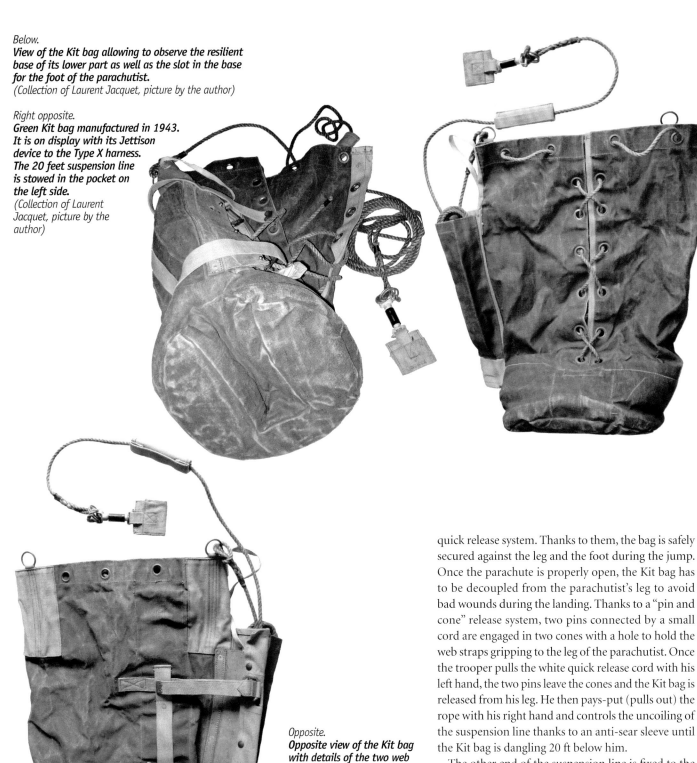

quick release system. Thanks to them, the bag is safely secured against the leg and the foot during the jump. Once the parachute is properly open, the Kit bag has to be decoupled from the parachutist's leg to avoid bad wounds during the landing. Thanks to a "pin and cone" release system, two pins connected by a small cord are engaged in two cones with a hole to hold the web straps gripping to the leg of the parachutist. Once the trooper pulls the white quick release cord with his left hand, the two pins leave the cones and the Kit bag is released from his leg. He then pays-put (pulls out) the rope with his right hand and controls the uncoiling of the suspension line thanks to an anti-sear sleeve until the Kit bag is dangling 20 ft below him.

The other end of the suspension line is fixed to the harness by a loop, then by a jettison device. It allows to jettison the Kit bag in case of dangerous entanglement with the Kit bag of another parachutist nearby or any other obstacle such as a tree or electric wires. On the side of the Kit bag, the suspension line is stowed and protected in a 37 cm x 8 cm pocket.

Above.
British parachutist on a C 47 Dakota equipped with a Kit bag. The higher part of the web strap that keeps the bag against the leg can be seen. Apparently, the parachutist is wearing motorbike gloves since he is deprived of any anti-sear sleeve.
(TWM)

Opposite.
Close up on an open Kit bag. The markings are visible, including the 1943 date of manufacturing, the DA 0020 manufacture mark and the Broad Arrow of the British War department.
(Collection of Laurent Jacquet, picture by the author)

Above.
Close up on the anti-sear sleeve used to slow the descent of the Kit bag at the end of the suspension line.
(Collection of Laurent Jacquet, picture by the author)

Opposite, from top to bottom.
Close up on the Jettison device of the Type X harness. It allows an emergency lowering of equipment in case of dangerous entanglement: close equipment of another parachutist, air obstacle such as tree or electric wires...

View of the pins out of the cones with the web straps loose.

In the « pin & cone » release system, two pins connected by a small cord are engaged in two cones with a hole to hold the web straps gripping the right leg of the parachutist. Once the trooper pulls the white quick release cord with his left hand, the two pins leave the cones and the Kit bag is released from his leg ; he then pays-put (pulls out) the rope with his right hand until the Kit bag is suspending 20 ft below him.
(Collection of Laurent Jacquet, picture by the author)

Opposite.
Nice picture of a parachutist dropped from a C 47 Dakota above Tatton Park. During this phase of the jump, the Kit bag is tightly secured against the right leg.
(IWM)

Opposite.
British parachutists at Megara, in Greece, on 14 October 1944. The men are indistinctively equipped with green harness with a painted QRB, or with a white harness. The second para on the column on the right is equipped with a leather straps Kit bag.
(IWM)

Left page.
**SAS paratroopers about to land.
The Kit bag hanging at the end of
the 20 ft suspension line is about
to hit the ground.**
(IWM)

Above.
**RAF C 47 dropping parachutists
above Tatton Park. Kit bags are
used during this training jump.**
(IWM)

Opposite.
**Training jumps with Kit bags at
Tatton Park in April 1944.**
(IWM)

KIT BAG USED BY SPECIAL SERVICES

K

Kit bag belonging to Lieutenant Maurice Geminel, a.k.a. Gerville, alias "Yen", assistant of Bunny Jedburgh team. Bunny team was composed with two British, captain Jocelyn Radice, a.k.a. "Peso" and radio operator sergeant James T. Chambers, a.k.a. Drachma. During Bob 256 operation, on the night of 17 to 18 August 1944, they were dropped on the "Amarante" DZ, near the Mont farm, between Boussenois and Vernois les Vesvres, 4 miles North of Selongey (Côte d'or), from a Halifax piloted by the F/L Green Abecassis of Squadron 161. The reception team was led by Michel Pichard (CL), a.k.a. Pic, a.k.a. Gauss. Captain Radice will be deadly wounded on August, 22, at Langres and Maurice Geminel will be injured on the 8 September near Latrecy.

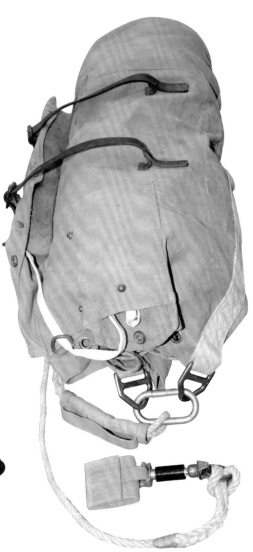

Opposite.
Kit bag belonging to Lieutenant Maurice Geminel, a.k.a. Gerville, alias "Yen", assistant of Bunny Jedburgh team. Bunny team was composed with two British, captain Jocelyn radice, a.k.a. "Peso" and radio operator sergeant James T. Chambers, a.k.a. Drachma. During Bob 256 operation, on the night of 17 to 18 August 1944, they were dropped on the "Amarante" DZ, near the Mont farm, between Boussenois and Vernois les Vesvres, 6 kilometers North of Selongey (Côte d'or), from a Halifax piloted by the F/L Green Abecassis of Squadron 161. The reception team was led by Micel Pichard (CL), a.k.a. Pic, a.k.a. Gauss. Captain Radice will be deadly wounded on August, 22, at Langres and Maurice Geminel will be injured on the 8 September near Latrecy.
(Collection et photos Bertand Souquet)

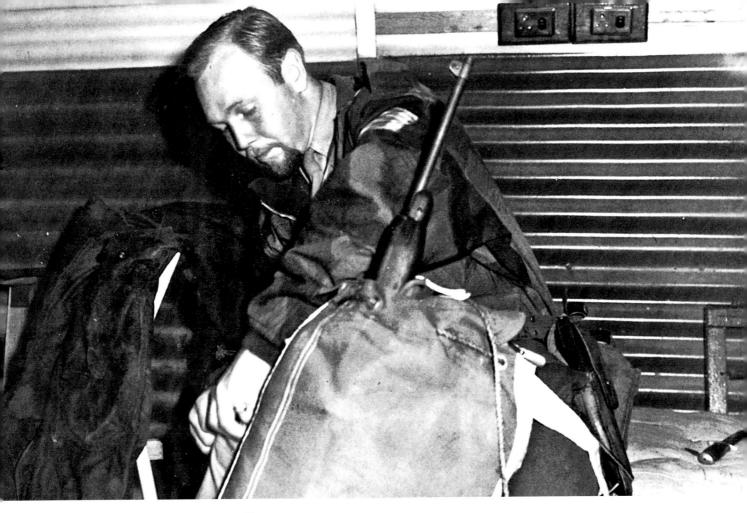

Above.
Jedburgh Team Ivor at Harrington. American radio operator 1st SGT Lewis Goddard a.k.a 'Oregon", buckles up his Kitbag whose pattern is very similar to Geminel's. The barrel of his M 1 carbine sticks up from his Kit bag. Notice the Denison Smock with an American flag on the left shoulder as well as the 45 ACP M 1911 A 1 pistol worn in a cross draw US 1916 holster.
(National Archives)

Opposite.
This kitbag, attributed to a French SAS, is of the same pattern than the one belonging to the Jedburgh Maurice Geminel. Yet it has to be noticed that the suspension line is replaced by a strap similar to that of the static line.
(Collection of Jean Bouchery, picture by Philippe Charbonnier)

Opposite.
US manufactured leg bag. This version was designed for Market Garden operation in Holland by Master Sergeant Joseph Lanci of the maintenance section of the 501 PIR para. It is very similar to the British version, with a 20 foot long static line instead of the suspension line, and a similar strap sewn around the pack to strengthen it. The pin and cone system is rather a deluxe version, with a handle and a metallic protection for a controlled opening parachute.
(D-Day paratroopers Historical Centers collection, Saint-Côme-du-Mont)

The lost kit bag of Roger Flamand during Dickens operation with 3rd SAS Battalion

Above.
Second lieutenant Roger Flamand in 1945. When the fights are over in Europe, Flamand joins on 7 July 1945 the Saint-Cyr Coetquidan School, where French officers are trained.
(SHD)

Below.
In October 1944, SAS sergeant Roger Flamand can meet his father and brother during his first leave in liberated France.
(Private records of Roger Flamand)

Roger Flamand was born on 4 December 1920 at Mégières in the Ardennes department. After finishing his training course to start a military career in infantry and having been appointed to the "Jeunesse et Montagne" unit at Vignemale in 1942, he escaped from France to Spain on 14 March 1943. Imprisoned in Spain from 15 March to 22 June 1943, he was set free and could join Casablanca in Morocco on 27 May 1943. After he volunteered in Free French Forces on 1 July 1943, Roger Flamand was appointed to the 3rd Air Infantry Battalion, to become the 3rd SAS BAT. Embarked for England on 25 October 1943, he landed at Liverpool on 7 November 1943. On 20 January 1944, he was qualified as a parachutist with patent number 3046.

First intended to be dropped on the "Bois d'Anjou" on the night of 27 to 28 July 1944 with Dickens operation, he was loaded with more than 22 kg of equipment spread between his different pockets. Unfortunately, the mission had to be aborted because the DZ had not been marked properly and the plane had to turn back. A second try was more successful during the following night. Taught by his first uncomfortable experience, Roger Flamand decided to unload part of his equipment to his Kit bag. But the bag could not resist the extra load and Roger Flamand lost it during his jump. Once on the ground, he had to start his war equipped with his 45 colt with 3 magazines and a Fairbairn dagger, only reinforced by a Sten gun and one magazine he managed to borrow from one of his fellow!

Sergeant Roger Flamand was dropped again on 7 April 1945 at Ruinen in Holland, during the Ahmerst operation. Later on, Roger Flamand would enter a military college and spend more than 20 years as a paratrooper in the Special Forces. Colonel Roger Flamand died on 10 January 2010, aged 89.

Picture taken from below of a parachutist wearing a Kit bag, hanging at the end of a 20 ft suspension line and about to land. (IWM)

LMG VALISE

The LMG valise, or Enfield valise, are based on the same principles than the leg Kit bag. It is meant to protect guns, such as Lee-Enfield rifle and Bren gun, with two variants, the Rifle valise and the Bren one. Manufactured with padded felt, the valise is connected to the harness by a 20 ft long rope hooked to the same jettison device.

Right page.
1942, this Norwegian paratrooper packs a Lee Enfield Rifle in a padded felt wrapping before placing it inside a CLE "Paratroops" container.
(Forsvarsmuseet Oslo)

Below..
5 June 1944 in England. Canadian paratroopers of the 1st battalion, awaiting to emplane to jump on D Day. Several Kit bags are visible, as well as a Bren valise on the ground on the foreground.
(Canadian Public records office)

Above.
17 September 1944, paratroopers of the 1st Polish Independent Parachute brigade are awaiting to emplane to jump for Market Garden operation in Holland. Several Kit bags are laying on the ground.
(Airborne Forces Museum)

RIFLE VALISE

Opposite.
On these two pictures, shot on 22 April 1944, the Kit bag and the Rifle valise can be observed in real situation. The main figure is Lieutenant Edward Vane de Lautour from 22nd Independant Parachute Company (6th Airborne Division Pathfinders), who will be one of the first to jump during the night of 5 to 6 June 1944. This Pathfinder is at the head of one of the sticks in charge of the marking of the DZ V. Robert de Lautour is deadly wounded on 20 June. On the first picture, the top of the Rifle valise is very clearly visible.
(IWM)

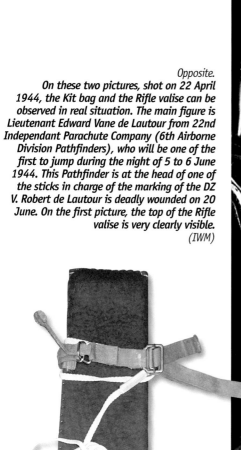

Left opposite.
Rifle valise ready for use. The suspension line is stowed in the web pockets designed for this purpose.
(Collection of Emmanuel Lefebvre, picture by the author)

Right opposite.
On the second picture, it becomes very clear that the officer is not only jumping with a Rifle valise but also with a Kit bag!
(IWM)

Right page.
British parachutists equipped with a Rifle valise and a Type X with a green harness and an unpainted QRB.
(IWM)

Initially designed for the wrapping and the protection of a Lee-Enfield rifle in the supplies containers, the Rifle valise is a plain trapezoidal felt blanket open on one end. Its periphery is roughly sewn and it is 44 inch long, 6 inch at the base and 8 inch at the open end.

It was modified by adding a web belt including a quick release system sewn at 8 inch from the top edge. Once the parachute is open, the trooper pulls the rip cord with his left hand, and controls the uncoiling of the cord that was stowed in an external pocket till his gun is dangling 20 ft below him. A small web strap with a "lift the dot" snap pressure at the top right end helps secure the weapon.

Opposite.
3,54 ft long Rifle valise, 6 inch large at one side and 9 inch at the opening side. The 20 ft long web suspension line ends with a jettison device designed for the harness of a Type X. The web strap has a quick release system.
(Collection of Emmanuel Lefebvre, picture by the author)

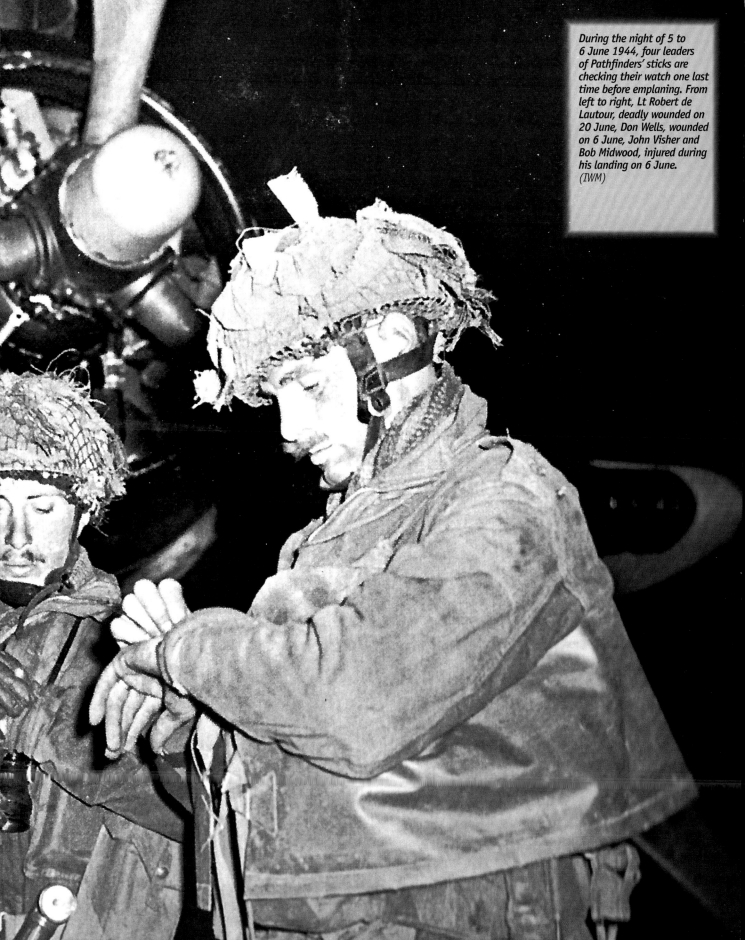

During the night of 5 to 6 June 1944, four leaders of Pathfinders' sticks are checking their watch one last time before emplaning. From left to right, Lt Robert de Lautour, deadly wounded on 20 June, Don Wells, wounded on 6 June, John Visher and Bob Midwood, injured during his landing on 6 June. (IWM)

Mk I Bren gun valise

It is designed on the same pattern than the case for Bren guns on supplies containers, and it is modified on a similar way than the Rifle valise. It is around 46 inch long and 9 inch large; sometimes a rectangular white label is sewn close to the end.

1942, two Norwegian paratroopers pack a Bren LMG in a padded felt wrapping before placing it inside a CLE "Paratroops" container. The Bren valises will be designed according to this pattern of wrapping.
(Forsvarsmuseet Oslo)

Below.
1942, these Norwegian paratroopers are placing Lee-Enfield rifles and a Bren LMG wrapped in padded felt inside a CLE paratroops container.
(Forsvarsmuseet Oslo)

MK II BREN
GUN VALISE

The Mk II valise is more elaborate than the previous one. Its flap allows a better security of the closing of the opening end. Its set of straps with a "pin and cone" quick release system is based on the same pattern than the Leg Kit bag.

Paratrooper sergeant equipped with the Bren valise. It is of major importance for the parachutist to get rid of this heavy valise as soon as the canopy is safely open and before his landing for he may be badly wounded. On the front, one can see the "pin and cone" quick release system that allows to decouple his neck and his leg from the valise. In his right hand he keeps an anti-sear sleeve around the 20 ft suspension line tied to his harness under his right arm.
(Airborne Forces Museum)

Opposite.
Detail of a poster showing a British parachutist about to jump from a C 47 Dakota. He is equipped with a Mk II Bren valise with its specific two web straps.

Below.
Drawing from the regular handbook « Equipment attached to Parachutists, Air publication 2453 A Vol I Part 4 Sect 2, may 1946 » with the details of a Mk II Bren Valise: pocket with flaps and two web straps bound by a "pin and cone" quick release system.
(Manuel Equipment attached to Parachutists, Air publication 2453 A Vol I Part 4 Sect 2, may 1946)

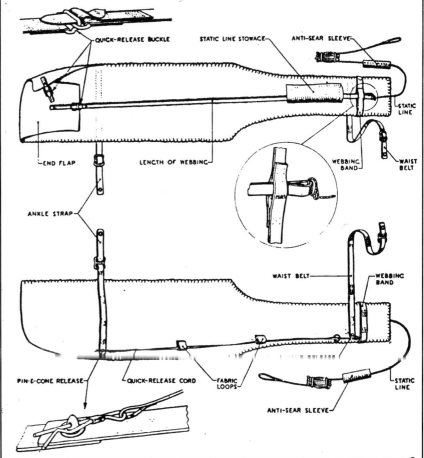

OTHER TYPES OF LOADING

Left above.
The specificity of the Airborne Bicycle consists in having a frame that can be folded in two.
(IWM)

Right above.
British parachutist equipped with the harness allowing jumping with the paratroops folding « Airborne Bicycle ».
(Airborne Force Experimental Establishment Ministry of Supply)

Opposite.
Handbook drawing of the Airborne bicycle packed for the jump.
(Airborne Forces Experimental Establishment - Ministry of Supply)

According to the purpose of their missions, the parachutists sometimes have to jump with different kind of pieces of equipment. They need then adequate and fitting valise.

• The quick release straps is a small multifunction harness that can be used when small material has to be carried, such as the pigeon case or the 26 ½ pds airborne folding bicycle.

• The airborne folding stretcher set is packed in two. The folded stretcher can be carried during the jump thanks to the combination of two quick release straps. The spare equipment (blankets, first-aid kit and dressings, digging shovel) is secured around the waist by quick release straps or set in a kitbag.

• The 303 Inch Vickers machine gun is also set in two during the jumping. The 40 pds Machine gun barrel,

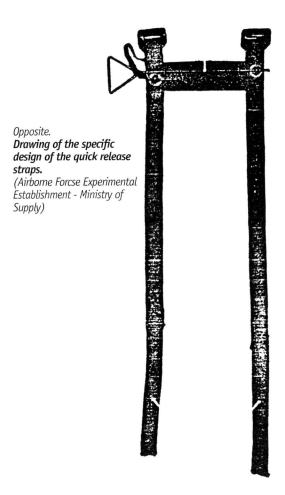

Opposite.
Drawing of the specific design of the quick release straps.
(Airborne Forcse Experimental Establishment - Ministry of Supply)

Above and below.
British parachutist equipped with a camouflaged Type X and Quick release straps that unable him to jump with a container for pigeons.

Close up on the system of the Quick release straps with a card container for pigeons.
(Airborne Forces Experimental Establishment - Ministry of Supply)

complete with action, is set in a Mk I Bren Gun valise and the 50 pds Machine gun tripod is folded in a kit-bag.

• On the same way, the 3-Mortar is spread in two during the jump. The barrel is set on a Rifle valise and the base plate on a Kit bag which can be loaded up to 60 lb with 15 lb extra stuff. The 2-Mortar Mk VIII doesn't need a special loading. Since it is only 21.37" long and less than 9 pounds heavy, it can simply be set into a Kit bag.

• The Projectile Infantry Anti Tank is 37,4 pds long and 35 pds of weight. The method to carry it is rather simple: the projectile support is undone and placed into a tube. It is thus coupled and secured to the jumping parachutist by a pin and cone quick release system.

Every heavy or cumbersome load is bound to the harness by a 20 ft cord, so that the parachutist does not have to land carrying it.

23 Septembre 1943   Leven.

«... Plonge tes regards en Silence
Dans le ciel pur de Ta Patrie!»

au Colonel SoSo Bourgii mon "Exemple" vivant
En souvenir de son Jour de fête ... - de do sorte de gloire. Jacq de la P.

Cdt de la Porte des Vaux

Capitaine de corvette Jacquelin de la Porte des Vaux equipped with a Mk I Type X on 23 September 1943. The picture is dedicated to colonel Bourgoin, commanding officer of the SAS 4th bat. "23 September 1943, at Leven. Stare in silence at the depth of the spotless sky of the mother land! To SAS colonel Bourgoin, my living model, in memory of this day of joy, on the edge of his day of glory. Cdt de la Porte des Vaux ».
(Collection of and picture by the author)

Paul Zigmant's QRB

Opposite.
Officer ID card of Paul Zigmant established at Calcutta on 11 April 1945 after he joined the Force 136.
Paul Zigmant, a.k.a. Paul Galet (1918-2007)
Demobilized in August 1940, Paul Zigmant quickly joins the French Resistance. In September 1941, he is one of the first members of Combat circuit. He becomes délégué regional of the area of Lyon where he settles all the frame of the Secret Army ("Armée secrete"). In August 1942, he is enlisted for the duration of the war in the French Fighting Forces ("Forces Françaises Combattantes") as a member of the Gallia RPA-Kasanga circuit. Arrested by the Gestapo on the 21 January 1943, he is incarcerated at Drancy camp where from he fails to escape. He is eventually freed on the 10 August 1944 and takes part to the Paris insurgency among the Chevrier Groupe Franc. Known for his organizer skill, he enters the POW and Deported Secretary of State ruled by Henri Fresnay, former head of the Armée secrète.
Yet Paul Zigmant decides to volunteer for Far East. He is appointed to the DGER in April 1945 and sent to England to follow a commando course at Milton Hall. Sent to India with the Special Services ("Service Action") on the 1 September 1945, he lands at Bombay by the end of September and joins Calcutta. He is dropped on the 20 October 1945 on Lakhom (Siam) with the second wave of the Kay II mission. Badly injured at the landing, with a double fracture of the pelvis, he is evacuated on Bangkok. In January 1946, hardly healed, he volunteers to join the 2d commando unit in mid-Laos, which he joins in February after a 105 miles walk. At Ban Nava, he becomes the effective assistant of Captain Rouget de Conigliano and takes part to the operations leading to the taking of Napé in April 1946. On the 16 June 1946, he is sent back to France.
Paul Zigmant dies in July 2007 at Pau. Officer of the Légion d'Honneur, he has been granted the 1939-1945 Croix de Guerre with two mentions, including one palm, and the Resistance medal with the rank of Officer.

Opposite.
Insignia kept by Paul Zigmant. A French title manufactured in Britain summons an unusual pair of Lieutenant Stripes since the French title is embroidered in silvered wire. British parachutist wings and Free French Forces parachutist wings come in addition to the general insignia of Free French Forces ("France Libre").

Opposite.
QRB of the Type X parachute used by Paul Zigmant during his jump on 20 October 1945 at Lakhom (Siam) with the second wave of the Kay II mission.
Paul Zigmant's QRB ref. 048103, used during Kay II mission
(Private collection)

THE KIT BAG AND FRENCH PARATROOPERS IN INDOCHINA

Above.
11 January 1948. 4th cie Mortar stick is gathered before leaving to jump on Than Nguyen province during « Teta » operation. The four first men are equipped with Kit bags.
(Collection of Jean-Michel Maïly)

Opposite.
A paratrooper of the 5th coy of the 2d SAS BCP is hanging on a tree to practice releasing his Kit bag once his parachute has opened. The training is organized to prepare the 1st operational jump of the 2 BCP in Cambodia in December 1947.
(Collection of Jean-Michel Maïly)

Next page at the bottom.
2 BCCP stick on the emplaning area. The troopers are equipped with US parachutes and locally made helmets of Bungey type. The trooper on the left holds a Kit bag.
(Collection of Jean-Michel Maïly)

Above.
During an operational Parachut operation alert, the corporals Lepage and Maïly are posing before a C 47 Dakota. Maïly is equipped with a US T5 parachute and holds a Kit bag before him.
(Collection of Jean-Michel Maïly)

Above.
In Indochina, at Dong Hoi, a 2 BCCP trooper equipped with a US T5 parachute and a green Kit bag.
(Collection of Jean-Michel Maïly)

TYPE X FOR BELGIANS PARAS COMMANDOS

Opposite.
1956, Katala DZ in Zaïre. This sergeant of the 3d Commando-Parachute Battalion of Belgium is equipped with a Type X parachute with a 1st type harness.

Below, from left to right.
Belgium commando paratroopers equipped with Type X heading to a DC 3 at Katala, in Zaïre, in 1956. They have put a small haversack at the bottom of their harness. The last two ones carry a container on their shoulder for heavy guns.

1956, Katala DZ, Zaïre. A Sergeant from the 6th squadron of the 3d Battalion of Belgium commando paratroopers is equipped with a Type X; his haversack, British as well, is hooked to his leg straps.
(Collection of Xavier Somme)

EXPERIMENTAL FLEXIBLE STEEL CABLE STATIC LINE FOR TYPE X, DEDICATED TO SPECIAL SERVICES

Ci-dessus.
Buick operation on 1 August 1944. 78 B17 of the 388 BG, 452 BG and 96 BG of the 8th Air Force fly over the Saisies pass (18 kms North-East to Albertville) and 7 men of the Union II mission are dropped with 899 containers on "Ebonite" DZ. The 7 OSS men (Major Peter Ortiz, Captain Francis Coolidge and Sergeants R. La Salle, Fred Brunner John Bodnar, Charles Perry and Jack Risler) jump with a Type X equipped with a flexible steel cable static line. The parachute of Sergeant Perry turns into a candle, causing a fatal landing.
(Picture by Raymond Bertrand, collection of Jack Risler)

This modification of the Type X with a flexible steel cable static line is only known thanks to the testimony of Jack Risler, veteran from the OSS Union II mission, who was dropped over the Saisies Pass in Savoie on 1 August 1944.

The members of the Union II mission were gathered and trained during one week on Knettershall airport (388 American Heavy Bomber group) where they were allowed one training jump and could practice with their guns. Having flied to London on a B17, they were briefed by colonel Buclanaster himself before jumping on 1 August 1944 during the Buick operation, a massive daily dropping. The mission suffers then its first casualty when Marines Sergeant Charles Perry's static line broke and his parachute candled, which caused his lethal fall at 14' 45". Risler and Perry were more than expert parachutists since both of them were monitors

Above.
1944 in England, John Bodnar and Jack Risler surrounding Charles Perry who will be killed on 1 August 1944 at his landing on the Saisies Pass.
(Collection of Jack Risler)

Left opposite.
1 August 2004, 60 years after their jump in France, John Bodnar and Jack Risler are made chevaliers de la Légion d'Honneur at the Saisies pass.
(Collection of Jack Risler)

at the OSS STS 33 jumping school at Holmewood Hall, near Ringway.

Upset by the fate of his fellow, Risler tried to figure out what had happened and wrote a report. It turned out that they had jumped with Type X British parachutes with a flexible steel cable static line. He mentioned that the pilots of the B 17, who were supposed to drop one parachutist by plane, were to slow down to 100-120 MPH. But, frightened by the proximity of the surrounding peaks (the Mont Blanc is no more than 32 miles away) they only extended the flaps, reducing the flying speed but keeping up the throttle. The back doors had been removed before the taking off in England to allow jumping, but they turned out to be inadequately narrow. The parachutists, heavily loaded with their equipment, had to ask the back gunner to push them out violently, which could provoke twisted exits. They all kept the memory of a violent and sudden opening of their parachutes. Risler estimated that the plane speed at the dropping should have been above 150 mph. According to him, Perry must have had a bad exit with twists, producing a loop that cut his cable static line 6 inches far from the apex. Jack Risler concluded that the crew must have seen what had happened and kept the remaining of the cable static line on the plane to have it analysed in case it might have been an act of sabotage. The dropping took place at day light and one of the resistant attending the scene from the ground could report that Perry twice tried and failed to shake his lift webs to open his canopy.

Above.
Parachutists preparing for a training jump at Harrington in August 1944. They wear a rather peculiar combination of Sorbo helmets and A2 leather flight jackets. On a closer look, they appear to be equipped with a Type X with a flexible steel cable static line.
(National Archives)

Below.
August 1944 at Harrington, other view from the briefing point. The parachutists are equipped with a Type X with a flexible steel cable static line. The cable stowed in the external pockets can be easily seen.
(National Archives)

The close studying of a collection of pictures taken at Harrington in August 1944 has made it possible to discover and observe several parachutists equipped with this kind of Type X with a flexible steel cable static line. Like in the Mk I, the outer pack has two external vertical pockets where the static line is stowed.

On these pictures, training jumps at Harrington can be seen as well as departures for missions on occupied France.

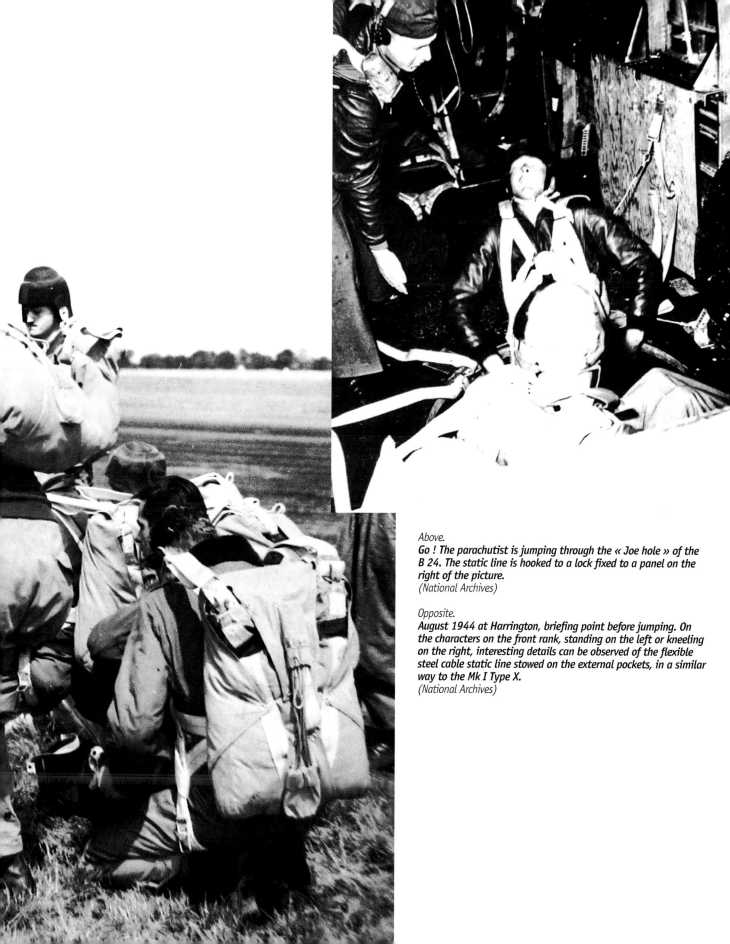

Above.
Go ! The parachutist is jumping through the « Joe hole » of the B 24. The static line is hooked to a lock fixed to a panel on the right of the picture.
(National Archives)

Opposite.
August 1944 at Harrington, briefing point before jumping. On the characters on the front rank, standing on the left or kneeling on the right, interesting details can be observed of the flexible steel cable static line stowed on the external pockets, in a similar way to the Mk I Type X.
(National Archives)

Above, from top to bottom.
Harrington, August 1944. According to the equipment the parachutists are putting on, they are likely to be part of a Jedburg or an Inter-allied mission. On the man turning his back on the left of the picture, the static line stowed in the external pockets is similar to the one on the Mk I Type X.

Picture taken on 11 August 1944 on Harrington Airfield. The members of the Anis mission are equipping themselves before going to the emplaning area. On the very left, the head of the mission, Michel "Pic" Pichard has almost finished putting on his jump suit. In the center, the radio operator Maurice Rosbach, a.k.a. "Sevillan", is turning his back, next to Cecile "Altesse" Pilchard, in charge of the coding. The members of the mission, led by Cecile's brother, will jump on "Hotel" DZ close to Rivière-les-Fosses in Haute Marne. The last parachutist on the right of the picture is equipped with a Type X with a flexible steel cable static line. (National Archives)

Below and opposite.
August 1944 at Harrington, Special missions parachutists equipping before leaving for occupied France. The men are equipped differently, SOE jumpsuit and Sorbo helmet for some of them, Oversmock, Denison and regular trousers for the others, which seems to indicate that they are heading for different kind of missions, Special for the first ones, and Jedburgh or Inter-allied for the others. The man on the front is putting on a Type X parachute with a flexible steel cable static line. A rectangular label of brown canvas is sewn on the right side of the harness and a similar rod on the top of the inner bag.
(National Archives)

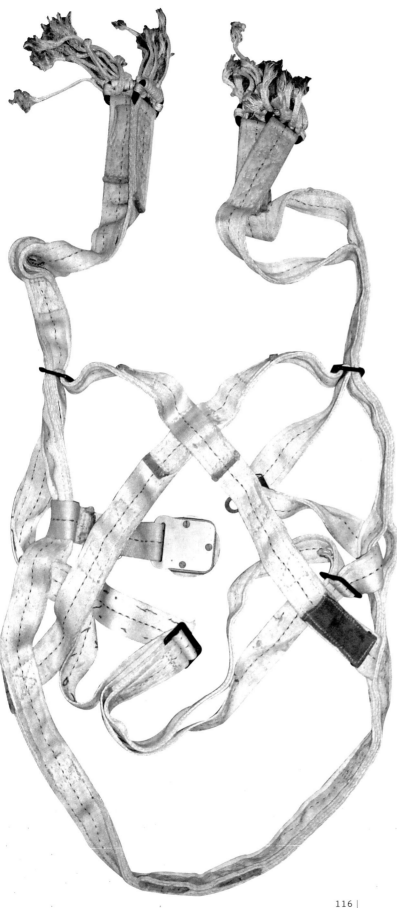

- First, so it seems, the Eon mission, dropped on 4 August 1944 over the Bonaparte DZ, near Kerien, 4 miles South-West of Bourbriac in the Côtes-du-Nord department;
- Then, positively, the Anis mission, dropped during Bob 224 Air mission. Three BCRA agents (Michel Pichard, a.k.a. Pic, alias Génératrice, his sister, Cécile de Marcilly born Pichard, alias Jacqueline, alias Altesse and the radio operator Maurice Roschbach) jumped during the night of the 11 to the 12 August, 1 miles far from Rivière les Fosses in the Haute-Marne department.

During these two missions the two kinds of static lines have been used during the same dropping.

During two other missions the flexible steel cable static line caused lethal accidents.

As it has already been told, during the dropping of OSS Union II mission, on 1 August 1944, the breaking of the cable line provoked the candling of the canopy, causing the death of Marines Sergeant Charles Perry. The mission was essentially composed with Marines that had joined the OSS: Major Peter Ortiz a.k.a. Chambellan, USAAF Captain Francis L. Coolidge (who had previously been a legionnaire, like Ortitz) a.k.a. Aimant and Sergeants Robert E. La Salle, Frederick J. Brunner, John P. Bodnar, Charles R. Perry and Jack Risler.

Opposite.
Second type harness found on the field from OG Christopher. A brown rectangular label is sewn on the right side of the harness.
(Collection of Charly Roussel)

Above.
11 August 1944, Harrington airfield. One of the members of ANIS mission is gently kissing Cécile Pichard on the cheek before heading to the dropping B 24. He is equipped with a flexible steel cable static line Type X and his harness has a brown rectangular label sewn on the side.
(National Archives)

Opposite.
Close up on the 3,54" x 1,57" brown rectangular label sewn on the right side of the harness from OG Christopher.
(Collection of Charly Roussel)

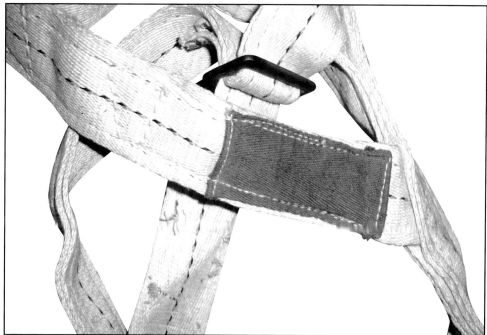

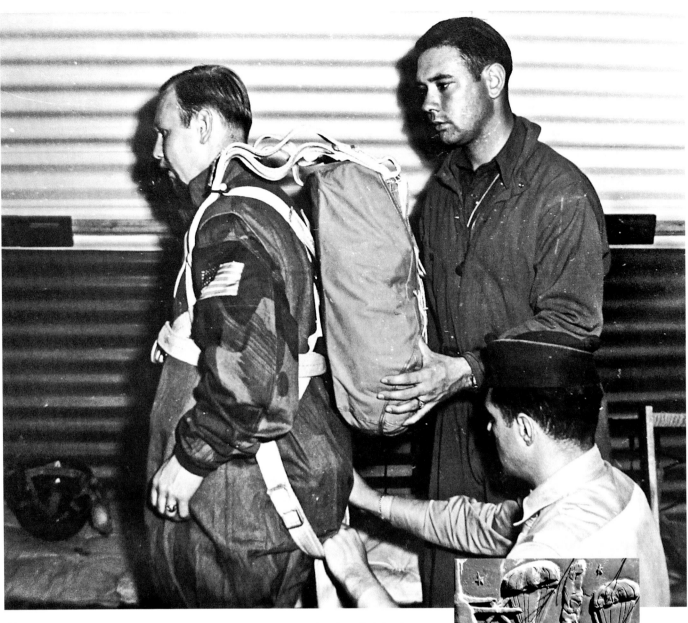

Above.
Harrington, 6 August 1944, Jedburgh Team Ivor. American radio operator 1st SGT Lewis Goddard, a.k.a 'Oregon", is putting on his parachute. On his Type X, a hook can be observed at the end of the flexible steel cable static line. This team was dropped on the night of 6 to 7 August 1944, close to Beddes in the Cher department. Goodard's parachute did not open properly and he was killed at the landing.
(National Archives)

The second lethal accident can be identified thanks to these pictures. The parachute of US Sergeant Lewis F. Goddard, a.k.a; Oregon, radio operator of Ivor Jedburgh team, has a flexible steel cable static line. Dropped on 6 August 1944 over the Paris DZ, 1 miles North of Châteaumeillant in the Cher department in the same time as British Captain John H. Cox, a.k.a. Monmouth, and French lieutenant Robert Colin, a.k.a. Yves Dantec, a.k.a. Selune, Goddard had his canopy candle, causing his fall and the fatal outcome.

Opposite.
Memorial of the Jedburgh Ivor team, dropped on the night of 6 to 7 August 1944 near Beddes in the Cher department. It shows the plane and the three parachutists on the air, including Goddard, trapped in a deadly fall when his canopy turned to candle.

C'EST ICI DANS LA NUIT DU 6 AU 7 AOUT 1944, QUE LE FIRST SERGENT AMERICAIN LEWIS GODDARD TROUVA LA MORT LORS DE SON PARACHUTAGE AVEC SES CAMARADES DE LA MISSION 'TEAM IVOR' . LES OFFICIERS DANTEC ET COX .

Above.
Harrington, 11 August 1944, Jedburgh Team Aubrey about to emplane the B 24 on their back. This Jedburgh team jumped on August 12 at 01:55 during Operation "Xavier" (Spiritualist 6 D for the RAF) near St Pathus Plessis-Belleville (in the Seine-et-Marne department). In the foreground: the British radio operator NCO Ivor Alfred Hooker "Thaler" and in back the French lieutenant A. Chaigneau "Koldare", a. k. a. J. Telmon, who was killed on 27 August 1944 near Oissey. One may notice that Chaigneau wears special Type X with flexible steel cable static line.
(National Archives)

Opposite.
Harrington, 6 August 1944, Jedburgh Team Ivor. Nice side picture of 2iC, French Lieutenant Robert Colin, a.k.a 'Selune". Like Goddard, Colin is equipped with a Type X with a flexible steel cable static line. The cable and the anchorage hook fixing it to the plane are very neat on the picture.
(National Archives)

POST-WAR MODIFIED TYPE X

After the war, two pairs of rings were added to the harness: the first pair on the higher part, allowing to hook a chest Type X reserve Mk II; the second one, on the lower part, for the Container Weapons & Personal Equipment Parachutist (CWPEP). History tells that the British paratroopers of the "Musketeer" operation, jumping on Suez in 1956, preferred to jump with no chest security pack so that they could carry more ammunition… The lower pair of rings that allows to tie a dinghy is missing on the post-war harness.

On the Quick Release Box, the side of the plate is cut straight on the left, so that the gripping is better and it is easier to check visually the actual position of the box, locked or not.

Above.
British paratrooper jumping from of a plane in Malaysia, between 1955 and 1960. He is equipped with a modified Type X with a white harness and a Type X reserve Mk II chest pack.
(IWM)

Opposite.
Parachutists putting on their modified Type X, with white harness and an extra double pair of triangular rings.
(IWM)

Below.
Rhodesian SAS about to emplane in the 1960s. They are still equipped with modified Type X with a white harness and a Type X eserve Mk II chest pack.

Above.
British paratroopers equipped with post-war modified Type X. Their harness is white but a double pair of triangular rings allows to fix the Type X reserve Mk II chest pack and a valise. The valise is of the same pattern that has been used during Musketeer operation on 5 November 1956 in Egypt.
(picture by the author)

Type PX1/I32/MK 2

(REF 15A/ 4177647)

PX M4 Type parachute during a jump on 7 May 2005 at Semnoz peak in Haute-Savoie department. The net surrounding the leading edge, approximately 4» broad, is one of the characteristics of this version of the Type PX.
(Picture of the association of the Dakota drop, 7 and 8 May 2005)

Opposite.
Type X parachute with a second version QRB. On the beige harness, a double row of rings allows to fix the chest pack and the supplies valise; another ring is dedicated to the potential fixing of a dinghy.
(Collection and picture by Stein Aasland)

Right page.
British parachutists equipped with a Type PX. The beige harness, an original one, allows to fix a chest pack.
(Airborne Forces Museum)

In November 1963, a new pattern, the Type PX, was adopted. Its look and its general design remained close to the Type X, but with several modifications:
- the harness was beige/khaki; from the beginning it included the two pairs of rings for hooking the chest reserve pack and the supplies container, as well as a low ring for the suspension line of the container.
- There were two variants of the PX4 QRB, broader and thicker than the ones of the initial Type X pattern:
- the look and dimensions of the first variant, manufactured in brushed steel, are almost similar to those of the Type X (3 inch of diameter and 1,6 inch thick). On the plate it still was carved "turn to unlock" and "press to release" in a half circle. A cross bar made it easier to check visually the position of the box (locked or not);
- a second variant, more recent, had bigger dimensions (3,2 inch of diameter and 2 inch thick). The central crossbar was in orange plastic. The "Turn to unlock" and "Press to release" inscriptions were painted in yellow letters on a black background.
- The PX QRB was always bound to the harness by one of the permanent higher lugs and never by a strap.
- The Mk4 PX canopy had 32 panels; it was bigger (32 feet of diameter) and its vented was covered.
- On the M4 version of the PX, the leading edge of the canopy ended in a 4 inch large net to avoid that the canopy may remain stuck and candle, causing an often lethal fall of the parachutist.
- The rigging lines of the Type X are white.
On the early 1970s, the Container Weapons & Personal Equipment Parachutist (CWPEP) was replaced by the Carrying Straps, Personal Equipment Parachutist (CSPEP Mk 2) with a 15ft nylon suspension line, more often known as the CPEP.
In 1981, a new chest pack, the PR7, was adopted. Easy to recognize by its red opening handle on the top of the pack, it included a spring extraction system and a bigger canopy, of 22 ft of diameter.

In 1993, the Type PX was replaced in turn by the Low Level Parachute (LLP) Mk I manufactured by GQ.

Opposite.
Front view of the first version of the QRB for the Type PX. The brushed steel plate has kept the appearance and almost similar dimensions to the Type X (3» of diameter and 1 5/8» thick). The half-circular carved inscriptions "turn to unlock" and "press to release" are stil in use. A crossbar helps to check visually the position of the box, locked or unlocked.
(Collection of Emmanuel Lefebvre, picture by the author)

Opposite.
Side view of a QRB for the first version of Type PX, registered under number 24161 with manufacturer's label AML 8 (Aircraft Materials Ltd).
(Collection of Emmanuel Lefebvre, picture by the author)

Opposite.
Side view of a QRB for the first version of Type PX, registered under number 24161 with manufacturer's label AML 8 (Aircraft Materials Ltd).
(Collection of Emmanuel Lefebvre, picture by the author)

Opposite.
Side view of a second version of a Type PX QRB. It is marked with its registration number Y 95872 and the manufacturer's label AML (Aircraft Materials Ltd).
(Collection of Emmanuel Lefebvre, picture by the author)

Above.
British parachutists equipped with a Type PX. The harness is beige with a PR 7 chest pack.
(Airborne Forces Museum)

Below.
View from below the second version QRB registered under number Y 95872. The inscriptions crossed by X are clues that the box has been modified to fit new norms. Reference 15 A / 1398 crossed and changed into 15 A / 1869. AML 11665 (ISS. 3 crossed and changed into ISS 7) MK.10 broad arrow MOD AML 57-61 and manufacturer's label AML 30 Aircraft Materials Ltd. PATS. APP. FOR.
(Collection of Emmanuel Lefebvre, picture by the author)

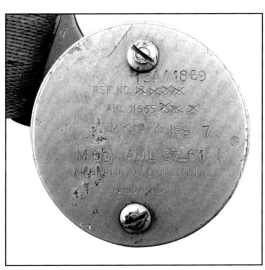

Above.
Commemorative jump over Semnoz pass in Haute-Savoie, on Saturday 7 May 2005. The parachutists are equipped with a Type PX4 parachute. The extension of the static line are easy to observe in the Dakota equipped with a "high cable" system, while it was a "low cable" system in use during WW2.
(Picture by the association for the Dakota jumping on 7 and 8 May 2005)

Opposite, from top to bottom.
Low angle shot of a Type PX canopy. One of the main differences with the canopy of the Type X is that the vented is open on the Type X.

Other view on a Type X canopy. On the PX4, the leading edge is surrounded by a net.
(Picture by the association for the Dakota jumping 7 and 8 May 2005)

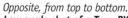

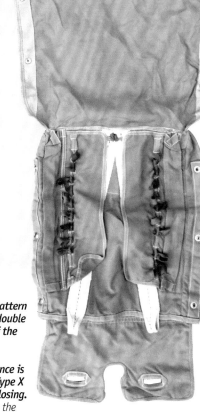

Above.
View of a parachutist equipped with a Type PX during a memorial jump on the Semnoz peak (Haute-Savoie department) on Saturday 7 May 2005.

Below.
Another picture in action of the other members of the stick. There still is some snow on the ground and the Annecy Lake can be seen on the horizon.
(Picture by the association for the Dakota jumping on 7 and 8 May 2005)

Opposite, from top to bottom.
Type PX Inner pack with the same inner pattern than the second version of the Type X. A double row of bungee cords allows the stowing of the gathered rigging lines.

View of a Type PX Inner pack. Its appearance is very similar to the second version of the Type X and its Newey snapper studs secure side closing.
(Collection of Emmanuel Lefebvre, picture by the author)

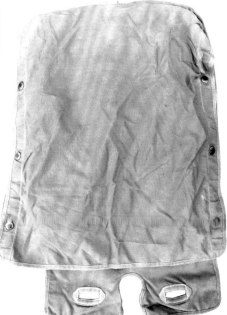

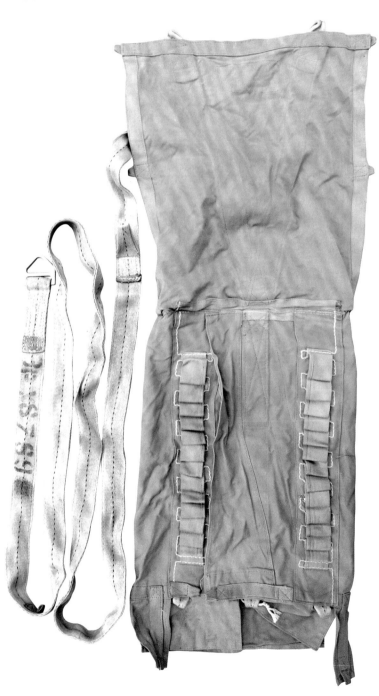

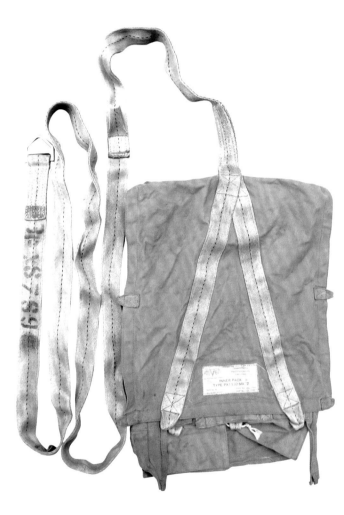

Opposite.
Type PX 1 Inner pack Mk 2 with its beige static line registered as 15A/1525. The rigging lines are now gathered into two parallel canvas stowing lines.

Above.
Type PX 1 Inner pack Mk 2 with its beige static line registered under ref. 15A/1525.
(Collection of Emmanuel Lefebvre, picture by the author)

Opposite.
Irvin manufacturer's label sewn on the Inner pack :
Pack Type . PX 1/I32/MK2
DRG/D.L. N°. IAC-D3749 Issue 8
Serial N°. Ref/NSN N°. 15A /4177647
Manufactured on the 10 November 1988
(Collection of Emmanuel Lefebvre, picture by the author)

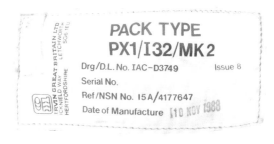

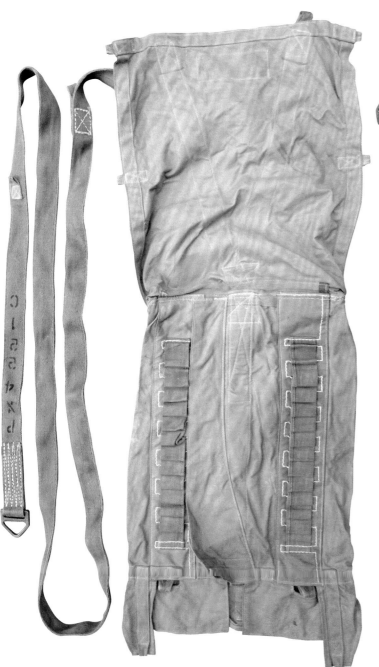

Opposite.
Type PX 1/I32/MK2 Inner pack Mk 2 15A /4177647, manufactured on the 10 November 1988. It is displayed open with its two parallel canvas stowing lines allowing to stowe the 28 gathered rigging lines.

Above.
Type PX 1 Inner pack Mk 2 15A 4177647 1988, displayed closed. Both its static line and its harness are beige.
(Collection of Emmanuel Lefebvre, picture by the author)

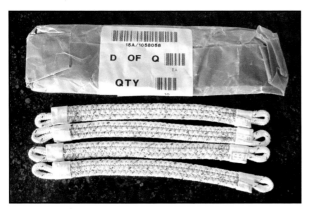

Opposite.
Pack of ten pieces of extension manufactured GQ ref 15A/1058058. Bar coding is a modern invention.
(Collection of Emmanuel Lefebvre, picture by the author)

Above.
View on the jumping out of the Dakota and the opening of the canopy of the Type PX parachute, May 2005.
(Picture by the association for the Dakota jumping on 7 and 8 May 2005)

Below.
View of the opposite side of the pack of ten pieces of extension manufactured by GQ. The reference (15A/1058058) can be observed, as well as the name of the manufacturer (GQ parachutes Ltd) and the date of manufacturing (August 1991).
(Collection of Emmanuel Lefebvre, picture by the author)

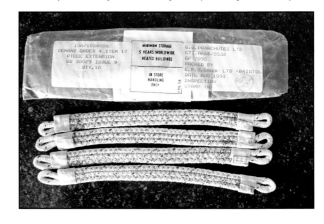

Below.
The tie of the Type PX is still very similar to the WW2 Type X. The marking of this one is GQ 111.
(Collection of Emmanuel Lefebvre, picture by the author)

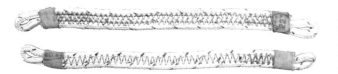

Opposite.
Two Type PX ties from different manufacturers. Slight differences can be observed. The first one is marked GQ 111 with a single stitching shaping a Z. The second one is marked P P 22 the Z is shaped by a double stitching.
(Collection of Emmanuel Lefebvre, picture by the author)

Above.
Picture « in action » taken by one of the parachutists, just after his canopy has opened. The Dakota is flying away and the following jumper is getting rid of some twists by shakings his legs.
(Picture by the association for the Dakota jumping on 7 and 8 May 2005)

Below.
Irvin manufacturer's label sewn on the pack of the PR 8:
Parachute pack
Assy Type PR/ 1
MRI IRV
Serial N° Co 265
Ref N°
Manufactured on 24 November 1978
(Collection of Emmanuel Lefebvre, picture by the author)

Opposite, from top to bottom.
On the PR 8 chest pack, the handle is on the right side and not on the top, the way it used to be on the PR 7.
(Collection of Emmanuel Lefebvre, picture by the author)

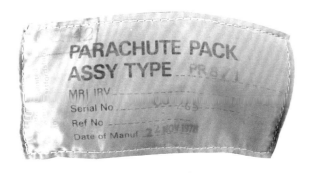

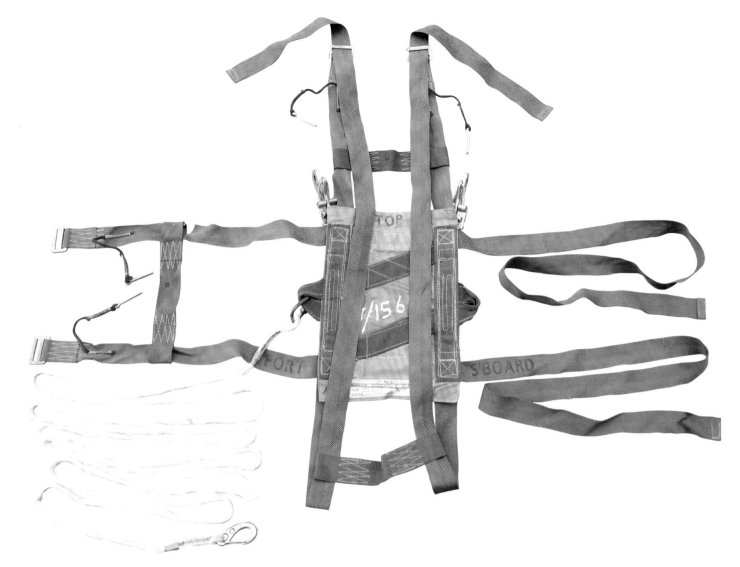

Above.
In 1964, the strap assembly « CSPEP » replaces the Kit bag. It is here exposed on flat, with its extension line.
(Collection of Emmanuel Lefebvre, picture by the author)

Opposite.
View on the rectangular plate of 10 x 1,2 ' from the CSPEP harness. The letters indicate the top of the harness.
(Collection of Emmanuel Lefebvre, picture by the author)

Below.
Label sewn next to the supplies harness, on the left of the British Army stamp (Broad Arrow):
M.E. Strap Assembly CSPEP
Ref N° Army A4/AD/1851. RAF 22C/2311
Manufactured on 26 August 1964.
(Collection of Emmanuel Lefebvre, picture by the author)

Opposite.
Mk 2 « CSPEP » harness with its suspension line.
(Collection of Emmanuel Lefebvre, picture by the author)

Opposite.
Back of a bundle made with a CSPEP Mk2 manufactured in 1981. The vertical pocket is on the center so as to be able to choose which side to fix the suspension line to.
(Collection of Emmanuel Lefebvre, picture by the author)

Opposite.
Picture taken in 2004 to commemorate the 60th anniversary of the Landing. Some mistakes have been made when it comes to a proper 1944 parachutist: the Type X is a post-war modified version, the side of the plate of the QRB is cut straight, and the rings fixing the valise and the chest pack have been added. And why would one set a Mk IV Sten under the harness when a Kit bag is available?
(MoD)

Below.
Detail of the quick release system crossbar on locked position. A red cord is tied to a metallic stick to keep the strap tensed.
When pulling the red cord, the metallic stick is set free and releases immediately the looping strap.
(Collection of Emmanuel Lefebvre, picture by the author)

HOW TO RECOGNIZE
A WW2 TYPE X?

The last variant of the Mk4 PX is not very different from the original Type X. But studying original materials of indisputable origin and pictures taken at the time provides us with positive elements that have to be kept in mind.

1- Most of the time, the WW2 harness are white, yet a few of them - those from the beginning of the war and those used par SOE and OSS- can be green or brown. On the contrary, at the end of 1960s the PX harness was manufactured khaki.

2- There's no ring to hook a chest pack or a supplies valise on the WW2 parachutes. It is only after 1955 that two pairs of rings have been added, the higher one for the chest pack, and the lower for the container.

3- The WW2 QRB plate was flat and round. After the war, it was cut straight on one side to help the gripping and the visual checking of the position of the box, locked or unlocked. The two versions of the PX4 QRB are broader and thicker than the initial ones.

4- The QRB can be tied to the harness by its own horizontal strap or by a permanent left upper lug. On the PX, only the lug could be found. Variants can also be found on the Inner pack, the rigging lines and the canopy.

5- After 1956, Newey snapper studs have been used to close the Inner bag instead of the breaking ropes.

6- The Mk4 PX had white rigging lines with a black fleck strand.

7- WW2 canopies had an apex and were composed of 28 panels, 32 for the PX Type. Usually they were camouflaged, reseda or white, but some were black. During the war, the canopy was manufactured with a special cotton ramex, or in nylon but never, never, with silk.

8- What about the AML manufacturer mark? The "Aircraft materials Ltd" cie, founded in 1957, has produced most of the Mk4 PX. They still used the AML mark but added the 1957 date on the lower line. Yet, some QRB of undisputable origin can be found with the same manufacture mark and only the numbers 5 or 12 on the lower line.

Above.
Dropping of British Parachute Battalion over Turkey. Their canopy they use is a first model of the Type PX, with no net around the leading edge.
(Picture by the association for the Dakota jumping on 7 and 8 May 2005)

Left page.
« In action » pictures taken by one of the parachutists dropped with Type PX above the historical "pen-sharpener" DZ at Vassieux-en-Vercors, on Sunday 8 May 2005.
(Picture by the association for the Dakota jumping on 7 and 8 May 2005)

Norwegian lieutenant equipped with a Type X parachute. On the sleeve of his Denison Smock, he is proudly wearing his flag and the wings of the British paratroopers.
(National Archives)

English parachute vocabulary

Anchor line cable	Cable d'accrochage (des SOA)
Anchorage	Ancrage
Apex usually call Vented	Cheminée
Bren Gun	Fusil mitrailleur Bren
Buckles	Bouclerie
Bungee cords	Elastiques
Canopy	Voile
Central line stitching	Surpiqure centrale
Chest Pack	Parachute de secours (ou ventral)
Chest Parachute	Parachute de secours (ou ventral)
Crutch	Soutenir avec des bequilles s'appuyer
Depress	Abaisser-compresser
Enplane	Embarquer
Flap	Volet,rabat
Gaiters	Guetres
Gore	Panneau triangulaire d'une voile
Harness	Harnais
Inner bag	Sac à voile
Jacket parachutiste	Blouse de saut modèle 1941
Jumpsuit	Combinaison de saut
Lift Webs	Elévateurs
Mention in dispatches	Citation
Outer pack	Sac à parachute
Pack (to)	Plier le parachute
Parachute Brigade	Brigade parachutiste
Plate	Plaque
Quick Release Box	Boitier de fermeture du harnais
Rigging lines	Suspentes
Static Line	Sangle d'ouverture automatique (SOA)
Tie	Estrope
to Jettison	Larguer
to mark the DZ	Baliser
to stowe	Lover (suspentes)
to unlock	Ouvrir la QRB
Type X or Statichute (GQ)	Parachute Type X
War Department	Service du materiel
Wrist handle	Dragonne

Type A	
Supplies pack	charge placé au-dessus du parachutiste
GEP General equipment pack	paquet-container aditionel
Jacob camouflaged cotton canvas	toile camouflée des supplies Pack et GEP
flexible steel cable	cable métallique souple

Kit Bag and Valise	
To secure the bag to the leg	assujetir le leg bag à la jambe
Resilient base	base rembourée
Rope	corde
Suspension line	corde de delestage
Quick release cord	corde du système de libération rapide du Kit Bag
Special cord release	corde du système de libération rapide du Kit Bag
Paying out rope	corde du système de libération rapide du Kit Bag
Felt	feutre
Valise	gaine
Rifle valise	gaine pour fusil
Bren valise	gaine pour fusil-mitrailleur Bren
Slot in base	passage du pied
Dangle below the para	pendu sous le parachutiste
Anti-sear sleeve	poignée de freinage
Special Quick release straps	sangle à ouverture rapide (Leg bag)
Jettison Device	Système de libération d'urgence (Leg Bag)
Quick release straps	Harnais pour petite charge

Study on the parachutes found on the field.

QRB				canopy	harness	sac à parachute	Operation		
Nomber	fab	painted	Type				date	country	
7452		green	Mk I	cam	green	cam (GEP)	19411010	France	SOE F General Equipment Pack
5823		green	Mk I		green			Norway	
M 32430		green	Mk II					Holland	
M 58649	AML 5	white	Mk I	White	white	Mk I white		Norway	
M 75843	AML 5	green	Mk I	cam	green	MK I cam		France	
		no	Mk I		white	MK II		France	South East
M 96570	AML 5	no	Mk I		white	Mk I		France	
M 048103	FBBC 2		Mk II				19451020	Siam	F 136 Zigmant
M 054753								Norway	
M 073932	DWCC 5		Mk I		white	Mk I	19440807	France	SAS Op SNELGROVE
M 116494				green	white		19450803	Laos	F 136 Dupau Raymond
M 133515	AML 5		Mk I				19440724	France	SAS Op Dickens, Capt Fournier
M 155934	DWCC II	no	Mk II	green	white	MK II	19440608	France	SAS Cooney parties
M 207087	AML 5	no	Mk II		white		19440904	France	OG Christopher
?		no	Mk I	?	green	?	19440107	France	SOE Ernest Henry Van Maurik
							19440207	France	SOE RF Camous
M 073779	BWCO S	no	Mk I		white		19440801	France	OSS UNION II
V 04770	AML 12		Mk I	black	white			France	
24161	AML 8		PX 1st pat		kakhi			GB	
Y 95872	AML		PX 2nd pat		kakhi			GB	

codes	parachute	Type	item	manufactur	autres marquages			provenance
15A/475	Type X	Mk I						
15A/495	Type X	MkI modified	outer bag					
15A/503	Type X	Mk II	outer bag					
15A/503	Type X	Mk II	outer bag	KMK				SAS COONEY
15A/503	Type X	Mk II	outer bag	WMCLL	36997			Norway HM
15A/4177647	Type PX	1/132/Mk2	Inner pack	IRVIN	NAC 42			
15A/156	Type C	Mk 2	reserve					
15A/381	Type X		harness	JBB	S 20802	J3 20		SAS COONEY
15A/429	Type X		canopy	KMK	26 44	AID. N.50	42	SAS COONEY
	Type X		canopy	WMCLL				F 136 Rossi
15A/429	Type X		canopy	WMCLL	34392	WMCLL 77		F 136 Ricard
15A/1398	Type PX	MK 10	QRB	AML 11665	ISS 3			
15A/1869	Type PX	Mk 10	QRB	AML 11665	ISS 7			MOD 57-61
15A/1525	Type PX	1/132/Mk2	Inner pack	IRVIN				
	Type PX		Tie	GQ 111				
15A/1058058	Type PX		Tie	GQ				
	Type PR8/1		Tie	IRVIN	Co 265			24-nov.-78
22C/2311	CSPEP				A4/AD/1851			20 aug 1964
	CSPEP	Mk 2		GQ 33	A4 8465			8 dec 1981

Donald OG dropped on 5 August 1944 at Guimiliau in Finistère (Brittany). The Type X parachutes have a green or a white harness. The two rifles are set in felt valise and the suspension line gets out of a web pocket. All wear a US M3 knife strapped against their calf. One can also notice the SOE knee pads and the SF wings worn together with the British parachutist wings.
(National Archives)